Free Play

Free Play

IMPROVISATION IN LIFE AND ART

Stephen Nachmanovitch

JEREMY P. TARCHER, INC.
Los Angeles

The author thanks the following for their permission to reprint from copyrighted works.

Constance Crown, for *Hands* by Rico Lebrun.

Walter Gruen, for *Musica Solar* by Remedios Varo.

Ben Berzinsky, for his photograph of a Carlo Bergonzi violin, c. 1770.

Grateful thanks to the late Arnold Fawcus of the Trianon Press, Paris, for permission to photograph his magnificent William Blake books.

Artist Rights Society, Inc., for *Two Children Drawing* and *Dawn Song* by Pablo Picasso. © ARS N.Y./SPADEM.

Charles E. Tuttle Co., Tokyo, Japan, for Tomikichiro Tokuriki's *Riding the Bull Home*.

North Point Press, for excerpt from Wendell Berry's essay, *Poetry and Marriage*.

For M. C. Escher's *Encounter* © 1989 M. C. Escher Heirs/Cordon Art, Baarn, Holland.

Excerpts from "Burnt Norton" and "Little Gidding" in *Four Quartets*, © 1943 by T. S. Eliot and renewed 1971 by Esme Valerie Eliot, reprinted by permission of Harcourt Brace Jovanovich, Inc.

Excerpt from *The Secret of the Golden Flower: A Chinese Book of Life*. Introduction by Carl Jung, translated and explained by Richard Wilhelm, reprinted by permission of Harcourt Brace Jovanovich, Inc.

Excerpt from *A Room of One's Own* by Virginia Woolf, © 1929 by Harcourt Brace Jovanovich, Inc. and renewed 1957 by Leonard Woolf, reprinted by permission of the publisher.

Library of Congress Cataloging in Publication Data
Nachmanovitch, Stephen.
    Free play: improvisation in life and art / Stephen Nachmanovitch

    p.   cm.
    Includes bibliographical references.
    ISBN 0-87477-578-7
    1. Creation (Literary, artistic, etc.) 2. Improvisation (Music)
I. Title.
BH301.C84N33 1990   89-49303
153.3'5—dc20   CIP

Jeremy P. Tarcher, Inc.
5858 Wilshire Blvd., Suite 200
Los Angeles, CA 90036

Distributed by St. Martin's Press, New York

Design by Deborah Daly

Manufactured in the United States of America
10 9 8 7 6 5 4 3 2 1

First Edition

Contents

The Fruits

*Paint as you like
and die happy.*

HENRY MILLER

Acknowledgments

The following are only a few of the many friends and colleagues whose support, criticism, ideas, and other contributions were vital to the creation of this book:

David Lebrun, Ron Fein, Abdul Aziz Said, Yehudi Menuhin, Ellen Dorland, Will McWhinney, Art Ellis, Ben Berzinsky, Jeremy Tarcher, Connie Zweig, Deena Metzger, Ruth Weisberg, Dianna Linden, Lolette Kuby, Linda Galijan, Sanjay Kumar, Jay Hoffman, Jim Bogan, Laura Kuhn, Elisabeth Des Marais.

My friend and teacher, Gregory Bateson, died three years before I began this work, but the power and warmth of his thought have influenced all of this in ways that are incalculable.

I am grateful to the Dorland Mountain Arts Colony, where the ideas here were conceived and sketched out in the composer's cottage in 1983.

This book is dedicated, with love, to my parents.

Prologue: A New Flute

A god can do it. But will you tell me how
a man can penetrate through the lyre's strings?
RANIER MARIA RILKE

There is an old Sanskrit word, *lîla,* which means play. Richer than our word, it means divine play, the play of creation, destruction, and re-creation, the folding and unfolding of the cosmos. *Lîla,* free and deep, is both the delight and enjoyment of this moment, and the play of God. It also means love.

Lîla may be the simplest thing there is—spontaneous, childish, disarming. But as we grow and experience the complexities of life, it may also be the most difficult and hard-won achievement imaginable, and its coming to fruition is a kind of homecoming to our true selves.

I want to begin with a story. Transcribed from Japanese folk sources,[1] it covers the whole sweep of the journey we will take in these pages. It gives us a taste of the attainment of free play, of the kind of creative breakthrough from which art and originality emerge. It is a tale of a young musician's journey from mere brilliance toward a more genuine artistry, one that emerges unimpeded from the very source of life:

A new flute was invented in China. A Japanese master musician discovered the subtle beauties of its tone and brought it back home, where he gave concerts all around the country. One evening he played with a community of musicians and music lovers who lived in a certain town. At the end of the concert, his name was called. He took out the new flute and played one piece. When he was

1

finished, there was silence in the room for a long moment. Then the voice of the oldest man was heard from the back of the room: "Like a god!"

The next day, as this master was packing to leave, the musicians approached him and asked how long it would take a skilled player to learn the new flute. "Years," he said. They asked if he would take a pupil, and he agreed. After he left, they decided among themselves to send a young man, a brilliantly talented flautist, sensitive to beauty, diligent and trustworthy. They gave him money for his living expenses and for the master's tuition, and sent him on his way to the capital, where the master lived.

The student arrived and was accepted by his teacher, who assigned him a single, simple tune. At first he received systematic instruction, but he easily mastered all the technical problems. Now he arrived for his daily lesson, sat down, and played his tune—and all the master could say was, "Something lacking." The student exerted himself in every possible way; he practiced for endless hours; yet day after day, week after week, all the master said was, "Something lacking." He begged the master to change the tune, but the master said no. The daily playing, the daily "something lacking" continued for months on end. The student's hope of success and fear of failure became ever magnified, and he swung from agitation to despondency.

Finally the frustration became too much for him. One night he packed his bag and slinked out. He continued to live in the capital city for some time longer, until his money ran dry. He began drinking. Finally, impoverished, he drifted back to his own part of the country. Ashamed to show his face to his former colleagues, he found a hut far out in the countryside. He still possessed his flutes, still played, but found no new inspiration in music. Passing farmers heard him play and sent their children to him for beginner's lessons. He lived this way for years.

One morning there was a knock at his door. It was the oldest past-master from his town, along with the youngest student. They told him that tonight they were going to have a concert, and they had all decided it would not take place without him. With some effort they overcame his feelings of fear and shame, and almost in a trance he picked up a flute and went with them. The concert began. As he waited behind the stage, no one intruded on his inner silence. Finally, at the end of the concert, his name was called. He stepped out onto the stage in his rags. He looked down at his hands, and realized that he had chosen the new flute.

Now he realized that he had nothing to gain and nothing to lose. He sat down and played the same tune he had played so many times for his teacher in the past. When he finished, there was silence for a long moment. Then the voice of the oldest man was heard, speaking softly from the back of the room: "Like a god!"

Introduction

Improvisation, it is a mystery. You can write a book about it, but by the end no one still knows what it is. When I improvise and I'm in good form, I'm like somebody half sleeping. I even forget there are people in front of me. Great improvisers are like priests; they are thinking only of their god.

STÉPHANE GRAPPELLI

I am a musician. One of the things I love best is to give totally improvised solo concerts on violin and viola. There is something energizing and challenging about being one-to-one with the audience and creating a piece of work that has both the freshness of the fleeting moment and—when everything is working—the structural tautness and symmetry of a living organism. It can be a remarkable and often moving experience in direct communication.

My experience of playing in this way is that "I" am not "doing something"; it's more like following, or taking dictation. This is, of course, a feeling that has been expressed many times by composers, poets, and other artists. There is the story of one of Bach's pupils asking him, "Papa, how do you ever think of so many tunes?" to which Bach replied, "My dear boy, my greatest difficulty is to avoid stepping on them when I get up in the morning." And there is the famous example of Michelangelo's theory of sculpture: The statue is already in the stone, has been in the stone since the beginning of time, and the sculptor's job is to *see* it and *release* it by carefully scraping away the excess material. William Blake, in a similar vein, writes of "melting apparent surfaces away, and displaying the infinite, which was hid."[2]

4

This book is about the inner sources of spontaneous creation. It is about where art comes from. I mean art in the widest sense. I have seen an automobile mechanic open the hood of my car and work with that special sensitivity of hand and eye, that deftness and readiness to absorb surprises, that quality of connectedness and wholeness, which we also recognize in a fine pianist, painter, or poet.

This book is directed toward people in any field who want to contact and strengthen their own creative powers. Its purpose is to propagate the understanding, joy, responsibility, and peace that come from the full use of the human imagination.

The questions we will delve into concern how intuitive music, or inspiration of any kind, arises within us, how it may be blocked, derailed, or obscured by certain unavoidable facts of life, and how it is finally liberated—how *we* are finally liberated—to speak or sing, write or paint, with our own authentic voice. Such questions lead us directly into territory where many religions and philosophies, as well as the actual experience of practicing artists, seem to converge.

What is the Source we tap into when we create? What did the old poets mean when they talked about the muse? Who is she? Where does the play of imagination come from? When are sounds music? When are patterns and colors art? When are words literature? When is instruction teaching? How do we balance structure and spontaneity, discipline and freedom? How does the passion of the artist's life get coded into the artwork? How do we as creators of artwork see to it that the original vision and passion that motivate us get accurately portrayed in our moment-to-moment creative activity? How do we as witnesses of artwork decode or release that passion when the artist is gone and we have only the artwork itself before us, to see and listen to, to remember and accept? How does it feel to fall in love with an instrument and an art?

I began writing this book as an exploration of the inner dimensions of improvisation. I found it inescapably fascinating that the conception, composition, practice, and performance of a piece of music could blossom in a single moment, and come out whole and satisfying. When I first found myself improvising, I felt with great excitement that I was onto something, a kind of spiritual connectedness that went far beyond the scope of music making. At the same time, improvisation extended the scope and relevance of music making until the artificial boundary between art and life disintegrated. I had found a freedom that was both exhilarating and exacting. Looking into the moment of improvisation, I was uncovering patterns related to every kind of creativity; uncovering clues as well to living a life that is self-creating, self-organizing, and authentic. I came to see improvisation as a master key to creativity.

In a sense, all art is improvisation. Some improvisations are presented as is, whole and at once; others are "doctored improvisations" that have been revised and restructured over a period of time before the public gets to enjoy the work. A composer who writes on paper is still improvising to begin with (if "only" mentally), then taking the products of the improvisation and refining and applying technique and theory to them. "Composing," wrote Arnold Schoenberg, "is a slowed-down improvisation; often one cannot write fast enough to keep up with the stream of ideas."[3] Finished artworks that we see and may love deeply are in a sense the relics or traces of a journey that has come and gone. What we reach through improvisation is the feel of the journey itself.

Improvisation is the most natural and widespread form of music making. Up until the last century, it was integral even to our literate musical tradition in the West. Leonardo da Vinci was one of the great pioneers of improvisation on the viola da braccio, and with his friends put on entire operas in which both the poetry and the music were made up on the spot.[4] In Baroque music, the art of playing keyboard instruments from a "figured bass" (an harmonic outline that the player fills in according to his fancy of the moment) resembled the modern jazz musician's art of playing over themes, motifs, or chord changes. In classical times, the cadenzas of violin, piano, and other concertos were meant to be improvised—a chance for the player to put his own creative display into the total artwork. Both Bach and Mozart were renowned as very free, agile, imaginative improvisers, and many stories, both moving and amusing, are attached to their exploits in this field. Beethoven, when he first came to Vienna, became known as an astounding improviser on the piano, and only later as a composer. Here are the reports of two musician-witnesses:

> I fancy that to these improvisations of Beethoven's I owe my most vivid musical impressions. I maintain that unless one has heard him improvise well and quite at ease, one can but imperfectly appreciate the vast scope of his genius. . . . His tempestuous inspiration poured forth such lovely melodies and harmonies unsought, because, mastered by musical emotion, he gave no thought to the search after effects that might have occurred to him with pen in hand.[5]

> He knew how to make such an impression on every listener that frequently there was not a single dry eye, while many broke out into loud sobs: For there was a certain magic in his expression aside from the beauty and originality of his ideas and his genial way of presenting them. When he had concluded an improvisation of this kind, he was capable of breaking out into boisterous laughter.[6]

Unfortunately, tape recorders were not available in those days. So when artists wanted to preserve their music, they had to be as deft with the pen as they were with their instruments. Mozart was perhaps the greatest improviser with pen and paper. He often wrote the fair copies of his scores and parts straight out, inventing the music as fast as the pen would go and hardly ever blotting a line. Beethoven, by contrast, intimately knowing the sounds he wanted, carrying them in his head for years at a time, could only record them on paper by the most laborious and energetic process of sketching, editing, crossing out, rewriting, and refining. His notebooks were a copious mess; through them we are able to trace, step by step, the evolution of his musical thoughts.

The rise of the formal concert hall in the nineteenth century gradually put an end to concert improvisation. The Industrial Age brought with it an excessive emphasis on specialization and professionalism in all fields of living. Most musicians confined themselves to the note-for-note playing of scores written by a handful of composers who somehow had access to the mysterious and godlike creative process. Composition and performance became progressively split from each other, to the detriment of both. Popular and classical forms also became ever more split from each other, again to the detriment of both. The new and the old lost their continuity. We entered a period in which concert goers came to believe that the only good composer was a dead composer.

Improvisation made its reappearance in this century, notably in the field of jazz. Later in the century, Indian music and other improvisational traditions reintroduced musicians to the pleasures of spontaneous creation. Beyond these forms of extemporization on a theme or within a set style, free improvisation and the invention of new and personal styles of art making are coming into their own. Today many artists are joining together in improvisatory chamber ensembles.

There has been a surge of free play as a modus operandi

in many other art forms, notably theater and dance, where increasingly improvisation is used not merely as a technique for developing new material in the studio but of presenting totally spontaneous, finished performances for the public. Visual art has had its tradition of "automatism"; painters such as Wassily Kandinsky, Yves Tanguy, Joan Miró, and Gordon Onslow Ford approached the canvas with no preconceived theme, but allowed the colors and forms to flow of themselves, from the spontaneous and intuitive promptings of the unconscious. In Kandinsky's breakthrough series of paintings called *Improvisations,* which set the stage for much of twentieth-century art, he saw himself tracing spiritual states and transformations as they occurred.

There is in all these forms of expression a unitive experience that is the essence of the creative mystery. The heart of improvisation is the free play of consciousness as it draws, writes, paints, and plays the raw material emerging from the unconscious. Such play entails a certain degree of risk.

Many musicians are fabulously skilled at playing the black dots on the printed page, but mystified by how the dots got there in the first place and apprehensive of playing without dots. Music theory does not help here; it teaches rules of the grammar, but not what to say. When people ask me how to improvise, only a little of what I can say is about music. The real story is about spontaneous expression, and it is therefore a spiritual and a psychological story rather than a story about the technique of one art form or another.

The details of any art form—how to play the violin, how to improvise a raga, how to write English prose, how to make movies, how to teach—are of course particular; each instrument or medium comes with its own language and lore. But there is a kind of metalearning, a metadoing that transfers across styles and forms; and it is that essence that I want to touch on in these pages. While there are certain principles that apply to a particular field, others apply across the board to all fields of creative activity. Any action can be practiced as an art, as a craft, or as drudgery.

How does one learn improvisation? Or any kind of art, for that matter? Or anything at all? It is a contradiction, an oxymoron. Here is the elementary double bind: Go up to someone and say, "Be spontaneous!" Or try letting someone do it to you. We submit ourselves to music, dance, or writing teachers who can criticize or suggest. But underneath it all, what they really ask of us is to "be spontaneous," "be creative." And that, of course, is easier said than done.

How does one learn improvisation? The only answer is to ask another question: What is stopping us? Spontaneous creation comes from our deepest being and is immaculately and originally ourselves. What we have to express is already with us, *is* us, so the work of creativity is not a matter of making the material come, but of unblocking the obstacles to its natural flow.

There is, therefore, no way to talk about the creative process without mentioning its opposite: the whole slimy, sticky business of blocks, that unbearable feeling of being stuck, of having nothing to say. This book, one hopes, can serve as a block-buster, a wedge for breaking apart creative blocks. But the process of working on blocks is a subtle one. It would be nice to have an easy set of recipes that we could apply: Seven Steps to Busting Our Blocks. Unfortunately, the creative processes do not work that way. The only way out of the complexity is through it. Ultimately, the only techniques that can help us are those we invent ourselves.

Nor can we talk about *the* creative process, because there are different personality types, and the creative processes of one are not the same as those of another. In the struggle for expression of the self, many selves can be expressed. Each of us must find his or her own way into and through these essential mysteries.

We have a right to create, a right to self-realization and fulfillment. Not everyone is in the business of standing up in front of an audience with no agenda, expecting the muse to arrive. But many people find themselves in similar positions. You may want to master a musical instrument, express yourself in painting, release the novel inside of you. You may be in school, wanting to summon up creativity to write an original dissertation; you may want to make a breakthrough in business, developing some new, unheard-of plan and executing it. You may be a therapist at wit's end over how to treat a client, a political activist searching for a more authentic way to tune people in to what is happening around them. How do you create a new way of managing a sprawling city, or write a piece of legislation to deal with some of the intractably knotty problems of state, nation, or world? How do you invent a new way of talking with your husband or wife or lover?

The literature on creativity is full of tales of breakthrough experiences. These moments come when you let go of some impediment or fear, and *boom*—in whooshes the muse. You feel clarity, power, freedom, as something unforeseeable jumps out of you. The literature of Zen, on which I have drawn heavily because of its deep penetration of the breakthrough experience, abounds with accounts of *kensho* and *satori*—moments of illumination and moments of total change of heart. There come points in your life when you simply kick the door open. But there is no ultimate breakthrough; what we find in the development of a creative life is an open-ended series of provisional breakthroughs. In this journey there is no endpoint, because it is the journey into the soul.

In my own life, music taught me to listen, not just to sound but to who I am. I discovered the relevance of our many mystical or esoteric traditions to the practical life of art making. "Mysticism" does not refer to cloudy belief systems or to hocus-pocus; it refers to direct and personal spiritual experience, as distinct from organized religion in which one is expected to believe secondhand experiences passed on in sacred books or by teachers or authorities. It is the mystics who bring creativity into religion. The mystic or visionary attitude expands and concretizes art, science, and daily life as well. Do I believe what "the Man" tells me, or am I going to try things out for myself and see what's really true for me?

Our subject is inherently a mystery. It cannot be fully expressed in words, because it concerns the deep preverbal levels of spirit. No kind of linear organization can do justice to this subject; by its nature it does not lie flat on the page. Looking at the creative process is like looking into a crystal: No matter which facet we gaze into, we see all the others reflected. In this book we will look into a number of facets, then keep returning to them from different angles as the view becomes deeper and more complete. These interreflecting themes, the prerequisites of creation, are playfulness, love, concentration, practice, skill, using the power of limits, using the power of mistakes, risk, surrender, patience, courage, and trust.

Creativity is a harmony of opposite tensions, as encapsulated in our opening idea of *lîla,* or divine play. As we ride through the flux of our own creative processes, we hold onto both poles. If we let go of play, our work becomes ponderous and stiff. If we let go of the sacred, our work loses its connection to the ground on which we live.

Knowledge of the creative process cannot substitute for creativity, but it can save us from giving up on creativity when the challenges seem too intimidating and free play seems blocked. If we know that our inevitable setbacks and frustrations are phases of the natural cycle of creative processes, if we know that our obstacles can become our ornaments, we can persevere and bring our desires to fruition. Such perseverance can be a real test, but there are ways through, there are guideposts. And the struggle, which is guaranteed to take a lifetime, is worth it. It is a struggle that generates incredible pleasure and joy. Every attempt we make is imperfect; yet each one of those imperfect attempts is an occasion for a delight unlike anything else on earth.

The creative process is a spiritual path. This adventure is about us, about the deep self, the composer in all of us, about originality, meaning not that which is all new, but that which is fully and originally ourselves.

The
Sources

Inspiration and Time's Flow

He who binds to himself a joy
Doth the winged life destroy;
But he who kisses the joy as it flies
Lives in Eternity's sun rise.
WILLIAM BLAKE

When we think *improvisation,* we tend to think first of improvised music or theater or dance; but beyond their own delights, such art forms are doors into an experience that constitutes the whole of everyday life. We are all improvisers. The most common form of improvisation is ordinary speech. As we talk and listen, we are drawing on a set of building blocks (vocabulary) and rules for combining them (grammar). These have been given to us by our culture. But the sentences we make with them may never have been said before and may never be said again. Every conversation is a form of jazz. The activity of instantaneous creation is as ordinary to us as breathing.

Whether we are creating high art or a meal, we improvise when we move with the flow of time and with our own evolving consciousness, rather than with a preordained script or recipe. In composed or scripted art forms, there are two kinds of time: the moment of inspiration in which a direct intuition of beauty or truth comes to the artist; then the often laborious struggle to hold onto it long enough to get it down on paper or canvas, film or stone. A novelist may have a moment (literally a flash) of insight in which the birth, meaning, and purpose of a new book reveals itself; but it may take years to write it. During that time he must not only keep the thought fresh and clear, he must also eat, live, make money, suffer, enjoy, be a friend, and everything else human beings do. In composed music or theater, moreover, there is yet a third kind of time: besides the moment (or moments) of inspiration and the time it takes to write the score, there is the time of the actual performance. Often the music is not even performed until after the composer's death.

In improvisation, there is only one time: This is what computer people call real time. The time of inspiration, the time of technically structuring and realizing the music, the time of playing it, and the time of communicating with the audience, as well as ordinary clock time, are all one. Memory and intention (which postulate past and future) and intuition (which indicates the eternal present) are fused. The iron is always hot.

Inspiration, experienced as an instantaneous flash, can be delightful and invigorating and can generate a lifetime of work. Giving birth to a line of poetry brings with it an incredible rush of energy, coherence and clarity, exaltation and exultation. In that moment, beauty is palpable, living. The body feels strong and light. The mind seems to float easily through the world. Emily Dickinson said in this regard that the poem is exterior to time. Improvisation is also called extemporization, meaning both "outside of time" and "from the time."

But this beautiful feeling is not enough. Like many other beauties and joys, it can betray us by appearing in one moment and vanishing in the next. If it is to result in a tangible artwork, or an extended improvisation of any quality, the creative inspiration must be sustained in time. And to do art only for the high feeling of completion and connectedness in the moment of inspiration would be like making love only for the moment of orgasm.

The work of the improviser is, therefore, to stretch out those momentary flashes, extend them until they merge into the activity of daily life. We then begin to experience creativity and the free play of improvisation as one with our ordinary mind and our ordinary activity. The ideal—which we can approach but never fully reach, for we all get stuck from time to time—is moment-to-moment nonstop flow. This is what many of the spiritual traditions refer to when they speak of "chopping wood, carrying water"—bringing into the humdrum activities of daily life the qualities of luminosity, depth, and simplicity-within-complexity that we associate with inspired moments. We can then say, with the Balinese, "We have no art. Everything we do is art." We can lead an active life in the world without being entangled in scripts or rigid expectations: doing without being too attached to the outcome, because the doing is its own outcome.

A walk, following your intuitive promptings, down the streets of a foreign city holds rewards far beyond a planned tour of the tried and tested. Such a walk is totally different from random drifting. Leaving your eyes and ears wide open, you allow your likes and dislikes, your conscious and unconscious desires and irritations, your irrational hunches, to guide you whenever there is a choice of turning right or left. You cut a path through the city that is yours alone, which brings you face to face with surprises destined for you alone. You discover conversations and friendships, meetings with remarkable people. When you travel in this way you are free; there are no have-to's and shoulds. You are structured at first only, perhaps, by the date of the plane departure. As the pattern of people and places unfolds, the trip, like an improvised piece of music, reveals its own inner structure and rhythm. Thus you set the stage for fateful encounters.

There are many situations in which we are inappropriately expected to plan or script the future. In particular, communication about human relationship tangles and twists when it does not come straight from the heart and straight from the mind. This is why we instinctively spot political speeches as fake. We tend to feel a little queasy whenever someone reads a prepared speech—even a very good one— instead of talking directly to us. If you are giving a public talk, it is fine to plan what you might say in order to sharpen your awareness, but when you arrive, throw away your plans and relate, in real time, to the people in the room.

In many schools, teaching is expected to follow syllabi that lay out what students will learn, as well as when and how they will learn it. But in a real classroom, whether kindergarten, graduate school, or the school of life, there are live people with personal needs and knowledge. A particular tap in *this* direction will shift this person's perspective; after today's discussion you know that *this* reading will be good to assign, based on what seems like the natural flow to the next step. You cannot plan these things. You have to teach each person, each class group, and each moment as a particular case that calls out for particular handling. Planning an agenda of learning without knowing who is going to be there, what their strengths and weaknesses are, how they interact, prevents surprises and prevents learning. The teacher's art is to connect, in real time, the living bodies of the students with the living body of the knowledge.

There are also plenty of settings that *are* appropriate for scripted behavior. If I am going to give an improvised concert, I leave to the feeling of the moment what and how I will play. But if I have announced the concert for Saturday night at 8:30 and people have arranged their lives to arrive at that time, then come hell or high water I will be there and be ready to play. And if that concert is to take place in a foreign city, I have no desire to encounter an improvised airline schedule!

A physician friend asked me what this ephemeral business of spontaneous creativity has to do with someone like him, whose work is practical and scientific. I asked back, "What is artistry in medicine?" He said that in hack medicine you regard what you're doing as an instance of a textbook case: You see the patient as a generic group of symptoms and try to classify him or her according to what your teachers told you. In real medicine you view the person as unique—in a sense, you drop your training. You are immersed in the case itself, letting your view of it develop in context. You certainly use your training; you refer to it, understand it, ground yourself in it, but you don't allow your training to blind you to the actual person who is sitting in front of you. In this way you pass beyond competence to *presence.* To do anything artistically you have to acquire technique, but you create *through* your technique and not *with* it.

Faithfulness to the moment and to the present circumstance entails continuous surrender. Perhaps we are surrendering to something delightful, but we still have to give up our expectations and a certain degree of control—give up being safely wrapped in our own story. We still engage in the important practice of planning and scheduling—not to rigidly lock in the future, but to tune up the self. In planning we focus attention on the field we are about to enter, then release the plan and discover the reality of time's flow. Thus we tap into living synchronicity.

As an improvising musician, I am not in the music business, I am not in the creativity business; I am in the surrender business. Improvisation is acceptance, in a single breath, of both transience and eternity. We know what *might* happen in the next day or minute, but we cannot know what *will* happen. To the extent that we feel sure of what will happen, we lock in the future and insulate ourselves against those essential surprises. Surrender means cultivating a comfortable attitude toward not-knowing, being nurtured by the mystery of moments that are dependably surprising, ever fresh.

Since the 1960s, the psychological issue of being in the moment has become a conscious preoccupation for many people. It came to be seen as one of the keys to self-realization, and variants of it are on the lips of a thousand teachers and gurus. The popularity of this idea tells us that we have touched on an issue of vital importance for our times; it crops up in every field from romantic love to quantum mechanics.

An empirical fact about our lives is that we do not and cannot know what will happen a day or a moment in advance. The unexpected awaits us at every turn and every breath. The future is a vast, perpetually regenerated mystery, and the more we live and know, the greater the mystery. When we drop the blinders of our preconceptions, we are virtually propelled by every circumstance into the present time and the present mind: the moment, the whole moment, and nothing but the moment. This is the state of mind taught and strengthened by improvisation, a state of mind in which the here and now is not some trendy idea but a matter of life and death, upon which we can learn to reliably depend. We can depend on the world being a perpetual surprise in perpetual motion. And a perpetual invitation to create.

Any good jazz player has innumerable tricks he can fall back on whenever he gets stuck. But to be an improviser you have to leave these tricks behind, go out on a limb and take risks, perhaps occasionally fall flat on your face. In fact, what audiences love most is for you to go ahead and fall. Then they get to see how you manage to pick yourself up and put the world back together again.

A creative life is risky business. To follow your own course, not patterned on parents, peers, or institutions, involves a delicate balance of tradition and personal freedom, a delicate balance of sticking to your guns and remaining open to change. While on some dimensions living a normal life, you are nevertheless a pioneer, venturing into new territory, breaking away from the molds and models that inhibit the heart's desire, creating life as it goes. Being, acting, creating in the moment without props and supports, without security, can be supreme play, and it can also be frightening, the very opposite of play. Stepping into the unknown can lead to delight, poetry, invention, humor, lifetime friendships, self-realization, and occasionally a great creative breakthrough. Stepping into the unknown can also lead to failure, disappointment, rejection, sickness, or death.

In creative work we play undisguisedly with the fleetingness of our life, with some awareness of our own death. Listen to Mozart's later music—you hear all its lightness, energy, transparency, and good humor, yet you also hear the breath of ghosts blowing through it. Death and life came to be that close for him. It was the completeness and intensity with which both primal forces met and fused in him, and his freedom to play with those forces, that made Mozart the supreme artist he was.

Every moment is precious, pre-

cisely because it *is* ephemeral and cannot be duplicated, retrieved, or captured. We think of precious things as those to be hoarded or preserved. In the performing arts we want to record the beautiful, unexpected performance, so we schedule a rematch for the camera. Indeed, many great performances have been recorded, and we are glad to have them. But I think the greatest performances always elude the camera, the tape recorder, the pen. They happen in the middle of the night when the musician plays for one special friend under the moonlight, they happen in the dress rehearsal just before the play opens. The fact that improvisation vanishes makes us appreciate that every moment of life is unique—a kiss, a sunset, a dance, a joke. None will ever recur in quite the same way. Each happens only once in the history of the universe.

The Vehicle

There is a vitality, a life force, an energy, a quickening, that is translated through you into action, and because there is only one of you in all time, this expression is unique. And if you block it, it will never exist through any other medium and will be lost.

MARTHA GRAHAM

Each piece of music we play, each dance, each drawing, each episode of life, reflects our own mind back at us, complete with all its imperfections, exactly as it is. In improvisation, we are especially aware of this reflective quality: Since we cannot go backward in time, there is no crossing out, editing, fixing, retouching, or regretting. In this respect, spontaneous music resembles Oriental calligraphy or ink painting. That watery gray-black ink on the brush, sliding over thin, fragile paper, does not allow a single mark or line to be erased or retraced. The painter-calligrapher must treat space as though it were time. The single-minded impulse from belly to shoulder to hand to brush to paper leaves its once-and-for-all trace, a unique moment forever frozen on paper. And the peculiarities and imperfections, which are there for all to see, are the mark of the calligrapher's original nature. The minute particulars of body, speech, mind, and movement are what we call *style,* the vehicle through which self moves and manifests itself.

The essence of style is this: We have something in us, about us; it can be called many things, but for now let's call it our original nature. We are born with our original nature, but on top of that, as we grow up, we accommodate to the patterns and habits of our culture, family, physical environment, and the daily business of the life we have taken on. What we are taught solidifies as "reality." Our persona, the mask we show the world, develops out of our experience and training, step by step from infancy to adulthood. We construct our world through the actions of perception, learning, and expectation. We construct our "self" through the same actions of perception, learning, and expectation. World and self interlock and match each other, step by step and shape by shape. If the two constructions, self and world, mesh, we grow from child to adult, becoming "normally adjusted individuals." If they do not mesh so well, we may experience feelings of inner division, loneliness, or alienation.

If we should happen to become artists, our work takes on, to a certain extent, the style of the time: the clothing in which we are dressed by our generation, our country and language, our surroundings, the people who have influenced us.

But somehow, even when we are grown up and "adjusted," everything we do and are—our handwriting, the vibrato of our voice, the way we handle the bow or breathe into the instrument, our way of using language, the look in our eyes, the pattern of whorling fingerprints on our hand—all these things are symptomatic of our original nature. They all show the imprint of our own deeper style or character.

It is sometimes thought that in improvisation we can do just anything. But lack of a conscious plan does not mean that our work is random or arbitrary. Improvisation always has its rules, even if they are not *a priori* rules. When we are totally faithful to our own individuality, we are actually following a very intricate design. This kind of freedom is the opposite of "just anything." We carry around the rules inherent in our organism. As living, patterned beings, we are incapable of producing anything random. We cannot even program a computer to produce random numbers; the most we can do is create a pattern so complex that we get an illusion of randomness. Our body-mind is a highly organized and structured affair, interconnected as only a natural organism can be that has evolved over hundreds of millions of years. An improviser does not operate from a formless vacuum, but from three billion years of organic evolution; all that we were is encoded somewhere in us. Beyond that vast history we have even more to draw upon: the dialogue with the Self—a dialogue not only with the past but with the future, the environment, and the divine within us. As our playing, writing, speaking, drawing, or dancing unfolds, the inner, unconscious logic of our being begins to show through and mold the material. This rich, deep patterning is the original nature that impresses itself like a seal upon everything we do or are.

We can see character by the way people walk, or dance, or sit still, or write. Look at the impulsive scrawls and hen scratches of Beethoven's musical handwriting, revealing the uncontrived defiance and integrity of his mind. Look at the flow and clarity of Bach's musical handwriting, revealing the uncontrived tidiness and roundness of his mind. Style and personality come through in every mark they made. Style is the vehicle of their great passion, not only personal, but transpersonal.

Or look at the powerful, free-spirited scribbles of Bach's contemporary, Hakuin, the great Japanese painter and reformer of Zen Buddhism, and his artist-priest followers. Some of the artwork we particularly remember them for are their *ensos,* those portraits of mind and reality that consist of nothing but an O, a circle brushed on paper with a single stroke. There's more to that "nothing but" than meets the eye. The character of that O, the variations and bends of the curve, its weights and textures, its wiggles and blemishes, reveal an imprimatur that comes from a place much deeper

Bach, above; Beethoven, below

than the style of the time, much deeper than technical ability or the surface of personality.

Virtually every spiritual tradition distinguishes the self-clinging ego from the deeper, creative Self: little self as opposed to big Self. The big Self is transpersonal, beyond any separated individuality, the common ground we all share.

William Blake made a curious and interesting remark: "Jesus was all virtue, and acted from impulse, not from rules."[7] We usually think of virtue as something that stems from following rules rather than impulse, and we usually think of acting from impulse as acting wild or crazy. But if Jesus had followed the rules of conventional morality and virtue, he would have died old as a loyal citizen of the Roman Empire. Impulse, like improvisation, is not "just anything"; it is not without structure but is the expression of organic, immanent, self-creating structure. Blake saw Jesus as the incarnation of God, acting not according to the fixed expectations of someone else's limited ideas but in accord with a deeper, bigger Self, beyond consciousness, the wholeness of the living universe, which expresses itself impulsively, spontaneously, through dreams, art, play, myth, spirituality.

This difference between impulse and rules was explained most clearly by e.e. cummings:

> *when god decided to invent*
> *everything he took one*
> *breath bigger than a circustent*
> *and everything began*
>
> *when man determined to destroy*
> *himself he picked the was*
> *of shall and finding only why*
> *smashed it into because*[8]

Those Zen artists with their simple O's had the knack of concentrating the whole of Self into the simplest acts. The spontaneous, simple O is the vehicle of Self, the vehicle of evolution, the vehicle of passion. It is the big, simple breath of God, uncomplicated by was and shall, why and because. As our flute player discovers, that imprimatur can never be studied or replicated just for effect. Hakuin wrote, "If you forget yourself, you become the universe."[9] That mysterious factor of surrender, the creative surprise that releases us and opens us up, spontaneously allows something to arise. If we are transparent, with nothing to hide, the gap between language and Being disappears. Then the Muse can speak.

The Stream

There on that scaffolding reclines
Michael Angelo.
With no more sound than the mice make
His hand moves to and fro.
Like a long-legged fly upon the stream
His mind moves upon silence.

W. B. YEATS

Let's return to Michelangelo's idea of removing apparent surfaces to reveal or liberate the statue that had been buried in the stone since the beginning of time. Michelangelo claimed that he was guided by a faculty he called *intelleto. Intelleto* is intelligence, not of the merely rational kind, but visionary intelligence, a deep *seeing* of the underlying pattern beneath appearances. Here the artist is, as it were, an archaeologist, uncovering deeper and deeper strata as he works, recovering not an ancient civilization but something as yet unborn, unseen, unheard except by the inner eye, the inner ear. He is not just removing apparent surfaces from some external object, he is removing apparent surfaces from the Self, revealing his original nature.

The ancient Taoists spoke of one's own being while in the meditative state as an "unsculpted block of time."[10] As stone is to a sculptor, so time is to a musician. Whenever he gets up to play, the musician stands there facing his own unsculpted block of time. Over this seemingly featureless void he draws, perhaps, a violin bow, which is a device for carving or shaping time—or let us say for discovering or releasing the shapes that are latent in that unique moment of time.

In the act of improvising we can do a number of things consciously. We can say to ourselves, This theme needs repeating; This new part of the material needs to be sewn together with the part that came a few minutes ago; This is horrible—cut it short or change it; This is great—let it grow; This feels like I'm approaching the end; and so forth. We're operating on a continuous stream of emerging pattern. We can modify the music, train it, make it more segmented, more symmetrical, larger or smaller. All these operations can be taught and learned. But the content, the stuff that is being operated upon, cannot be taught or learned. It is simply there to be seen, heard, felt, not by the five senses but by some faculty that resembles *intelleto.*

What, then, *is* this seemingly endless stream of music, dance, imagery, acting, or speech that comes out of us whenever we let it? To some extent it is the stream of consciousness, a river of memories, fragments of melodies, emotions, fragrances, angers, old loves, fantasies. But we sense something else, beyond the personal, from a source that is both very old and very new. The raw material is a kind of flow—Herakleitos' river of time, or the great Tao, flowing through us, as us. Mysteriously flowing through, unstoppable and unstartable. At its source, it does not appear or disappear, does not increase or decrease, is neither tainted nor pure. We can choose to tap into it or not to tap into it; we can find ourselves unwillingly opened up to it or unwillingly cut off from it. But it's always there.

Spiritual traditions the world over are full of references to this mysterious juice: *ch'i* in China and *ki* in Japan (embodying the great Tao in each individual); *kundalini* and *prana* in India; *mana* in Polynesia; *orendé* and *manitu* among the Iroquois and Algonquins; *axé* among the Afro-Brazilian *condomblé* cults; *baraka* among the Sufis in the Middle East; *élan vital* on the streets of Paris. The common theme is that the person is a vessel or conduit through which a transpersonal force flows. That force can be enhanced through practice and discipline of various sorts; it can become blocked or bottled up through neglect, poor practice, or fear; it can be used for good or evil; it flows through us, yet we do not own it; it appears as a principal factor in the arts, in healing, in religion.

Listening now to the Pablo Casals recordings of the Bach *Cello Suites,* made half a century ago in the mid 1930s, I feel a quality to the sound itself that goes right *through* me. It vibrates my whole body like a leaf in a storm. I don't know what to call it—power, the life force. To use terms like *force* or *energy* can be misleading, however, because we are not referring to physical energy in the sense of mass times velocity squared, or to the metabolic energy that the body derives from food. Yet anyone who, like a musician, deals with these matters on a practical day-to-day basis knows that to consider this phenomenon nothing but a metaphor is to make an equally great error.

What the shamans, artists, healers, and musicians are talking about is not a force or energy, though it is expressed or carried by fluctuations of energy (just as music is carried on the fluctuations of sound waves or radio waves). It is not in the realm of energy but in the realm of information, of *pattern.*

Looking out, now, over the ocean, the birds, the vegetation, I see that absolutely everything in nature arises from the power of free play sloshing against the power of limits. The limits may be intricate, subtle, and long-lived like the genetic structure of the orange tree before me. But the pattern of the ocean, the pattern of the orange tree or the sea gulls, arises organically; it is a self-organizing pattern. The self-organizing activity arises, slowly changes, suddenly shifts, learns from mistakes, interacts with the ways of its fellows and its environment. These creative processes inherent in nature are called by some people evolution, by others creation. The unending flow through time and space of this pattern of patterns is what the Chinese call the Tao.

In myths the world over, the creator-gods, making do with what simple materials they have at hand—water, fire, moonlight, mud—improvise the land and sea, the world of animal and plant, human society, the arts, the cosmos, and history. These creative processes are a paradigm for how our own creative processes work at those especially beautiful moments when the work flows and work is play and the process and the product are one.

The Creative and the Receptive, making and sensing, are a resonant pair, matching and answering each other. Michelangelo, in surrendering to the archetypal shapes latent in his stone, did not make statues, he released them. He consciously followed Plato's idea that learning is really re-membering. In the dialogue *Meno,* for example, Plato shows how Socrates releases from a supposedly ignorant slave the

most abstruse knowledge of mathematics and philosophy by asking the right questions in the right way. That deep innate patterning of information is holographically present in whatever we care to look at; not just in Michelangelo's blocks of Carrara marble, but in everything, in us-interacting-with-everything, us-reflective-of-everything. It is as if there were something underneath this piece of paper, a pattern whose outline I am trying to catch and make visible by pointing to it with these words.

Our sculpture metaphor should not trap us into thinking that *intelleto* is seeing into a static or ideal essence. The knowledge we tap into is *intelleto* of a dynamic reality in constant flux—a flux that is not random but is in itself a pattern of patterns. When we experience inspiration, be it in love, in invention, in music, in writing, in business, in sport, in meditation, we are tuning into this ever-present, ever-changing environment of information about the deep structure of our world, this ever-flowing Tao.

The Muse

To the rationally minded, the mental process of the intuitive appears to work backward. His conclusions are reached before his premises. This is not because the steps which connect the two have been omitted but because those steps are taken by the unconscious.

FRANCES WICKES

To be infinitely sensitive to the sound, sight, and feel of the work in front of us is to listen for our intuitive voice—our Muse, as she used to be called, or Genius, as he used to be called. The Romans believed that we each have our "genius," a familial deity or spirit guide. Our genius senses and reflects what is around us; we transform matter, time, and space through our own original being.

The source of creative inspiration has been variously identified in the world's cultures as a woman, a man, or a child. The female muse is a figure we are familiar with from the ninefold Muses of Greek mythology and from the post-Renaissance poets. Her roots stretch back beyond humanity to the Earth Mother. She is the goddess of wisdom, Sophia. The male muse appears as the Sufi figure Khidr or as Blake's vigorous blacksmith-prophet-sungod, Los. The child muse is the allegorical figure of Play.

In Blake's watercolor *Bright-Eyed Fancy,* we see a young woman hovering over a poet-musician playing his lyre. She is pouring out a cornucopia full of ideas in the form of pixies and babies, which the poet-musician tries to play—almost as if his lyre were an instrument for taking notes—before they evaporate into thin air.

Khidr was personified by the Sufis as a man in a luminous green robe, the secret guide who whispered in the ear of Moses and the other prophets, who can appear to any of us at the moment of need, when our tongues need freeing. The green robe is not cloth; it is Earth's real vegetation. Khidr is known as the "Verdant One," and as such he holds many of the attributes that we in the West associate with both the Muse and the Earth Mother. Male or female, the voice of the biosphere wells up within us, whispering urgent messages from the depths. Khidr is the "green gold" that the alchemists were trying to make, the color of foliage with sunlight shining through it. This color is the blending of earthly and celestial life. It is neither an abstraction nor a mystical dream, but the everyday chemistry of photosynthesis by which we live.

Each image of the muse illuminates one of the infinitely many shapes that creativity can take. Here is a different one: Imagine how you might feel about your writing if instead of typing it on a computer or writing longhand you were dictating it to a baby elephant holding a stylus in his trunk. In India there is a god called Ganesh, who is half boy, half elephant. The ancient bards of India were, like Homer, illiterate, but Ganesh could read and write, and he served as secretary to the poets. India's immense epic, the *Mahabharata,* was dictated by the poet Vyasa to Ganesh. Ganesh agreed to write down this poem, thirteen times longer than the Bible, on the condition that Vyasa never stop improvising his verses until the whole gigantic tale was finished. Vyasa agreed on condition that Ganesh write only what he could understand. If Ganesh did not understand something, he had to pause and think about it until he did. We conventionally think of the Muse as the eternal source of inspiration that the poet channels, but the Ganesh myth inverts the relationship. It shows us inspiration coming straight from the poet's heart, needing no explanation, no proof, no godlike source; while the mys-

tery to be explained is technique (*techne* from the Greek for "art"). The godlike phenomenon is not the inspiration but the craft by which the inspiration is realized.

Muses live not just in myth and legend, but in our day-to-day existence as well. We are free to invent our own muses as needed. Some friends and I formed a music-dance-theater improvisation group called the Congregation. One day we were congregating in the studio, completely blocked on the creative work we had set out to do together, each of us angry about various frustrations that were piling up in our lives. Then Terry Sendgraff found an old, cracked green tennis ball in a corner of the floor. She picked it up and squeezed it. The crack in one side popped open and shut as she kept squeezing. The upper edge of the crack sported a protrusion that flipped in and out with a thwacking noise as the mouth opened and closed, just like a big broken tooth. Suddenly Snaggletooth was born. As she worked the tennis ball, Terry began speaking in Snaggletooth's old, humorous, high-pitched voice. Snaggletooth told us to calm down, not to worry about being stuck in our work. She promised to tell us what to do—and she did. She restored our good feelings and then dictated a wonderful piece of art. Terry had split into a muse plus her ordinary self. The muse, representing a bigger entity than self, was not Terry's personal muse, but our group muse. We took turns operating Snaggletooth, but the voice, personality, and authoritativeness remained the same. She continued to speak better and more clearly than we bumbling humans could manage to. We soon began calling her Snaggletruth, with a mixture of humor and heartfelt gratitude.

Although Snaggletooth has long since disappeared, one can consider this volume to be the first book of aesthetics and philosophy to be dictated by a tennis ball.

That green ball of the Earth, the biosphere, the Verdant One, is the big entity of which we are part; and the Muse, or Khidr, Sophia, or the Holy Spirit, is the voice of the whole speaking through the parts. This voice speaks a language that we find often incomprehensible, sometimes even frightening—and always awesome.

The muse is the living voice, as each of us experiences it, of intuition. Intuition is a synaptic summation, our whole nervous system balancing and combining multivariate complexities in a single flash. It's like computation; but while computation is a lineal process, going from A to B to C, intuition computes concentrically. All the steps and variables converge on the central decision-point at once, which is the present moment.

Reasoned knowledge proceeds one step at a time, and the results of one step can, and often do, overturn the results of the previous step—hence, those moments when we think too much and can't firmly decide what to do. Reasoned knowledge proceeds from information of which we're consciously aware—only a partial sampling of our total knowledge. Intuitive knowledge, on the other hand, proceeds from everything we know and everything we are. It converges on the moment from a rich plurality of directions and sources—hence the feeling of absolute certainty that is traditionally associated with intuitive knowledge.

Pascal said, "The heart has its reasons, which reason cannot know."[11] Feeling has its own structure, just as thinking has its own structure. There are levels of feeling, and levels of thinking, and something deeper than both of them, something that is feeling and thought and both and neither. When we speak of "trusting your gut," it is to this activity, intuition, that we are referring our decisions.

I remember a feeling that caught me as I hung up the telephone once, a kind of sadness. I realized that my inner knowing had told me to say something, and I did not pay attention. I thought, with regret, back to other times when I had heard that voice and ignored it. The simplest yet most elusive lesson in life is learning to listen to that guiding voice. I've learned to respond to it more and more, yet the times still come when I admit that I have just missed some extraordinary experience because I failed to catch the message fast enough. And when that happens, something is irrevocably lost. It is vital at such moments to learn how to forgive oneself. Perhaps the awakened state means being ever ready to respond—something that no one can be all the time. But we can approach it; we can learn to listen more and more reliably. Mastery means responsibility, ability to respond in real time to the need of the moment. Intuitive or inspired living means not just passively hearing the voice, but acting on it.

Improvisation is intuition in action, a way to discover the muse and learn to respond to her call. Even if we work in a very structured, compositional way, we begin by that always surprising process of free invention in which we have nothing to gain and nothing to lose. The outpourings of intuition consist of a continuous, rapid flow of choice, choice, choice, choice. When we improvise with the whole heart, riding this flow, the choices and images open into each other so rapidly that we have no time to get scared and retreat from what intuition is telling us.

The whole essence of bringing art into life is learning to listen to that guiding voice. Opening up the violin case and picking up the instrument is, for me, a context marker, a clear message to myself: "Now it's time to respond to that voice." Because that moment is so marked, it is easy to tune in. The far greater challenge is to bring that poetic cognizance into daily life.

Finding the heart's voice—that is the adventure at the core of this book. That is what every artist is dedicated to: the lifelong quest—not a vision quest, for vision is all around us—but our quest to learn to speak with our own voice.

Mind at Play

*The creation of something new is not accomplished
by the intellect but by the play instinct acting from
inner necessity. The creative mind plays with the
objects it loves.*

CARL JUNG

Improvisation, composition, writing, painting, theater, invention, all creative acts are forms of play, the starting
place of creativity in the human growth cycle, and one of the
great primal life functions. Without play, learning and evolution are impossible. Play is the taproot from which original
art springs; it is the raw stuff that the artist channels and
organizes with all his learning and technique. Technique
itself springs from play, because we can acquire technique
only by the practice of practice, by persistently experimenting and playing with our tools and testing their limits and
resistances. Creative work is play; it is free speculation using
the materials of one's chosen form. The creative mind plays
with the objects it loves. Artists play with color and space.
Musicians play with sound and silence. Eros plays with lovers. Gods play with the universe. Children play with everything they can get their hands on.

Play is ubiquitous among the higher mammals and rampant among monkeys and apes. Among humans, as Johan
Huizinga has shown in *Homo Ludens: A Study of the Play Element in Culture,* play pervades every facet of our life and has
proliferated into all sorts of highly evolved forms, such as
ritual, the arts, statecraft, sports, and civilization itself. "But
in acknowledging play," writes Huizinga, "you acknowledge mind, for whatever play is, it is not matter."[12]

42

Play is always a matter of context. It is not what we do, but how we do it. Play cannot be defined, because in play all definitions slither, dance, combine, break apart, and recombine. The mood of play can be impish or supremely solemn. When the most challenging labors are undertaken from the joyous work spirit, they are play. In play we manifest fresh, interactive ways of relating with people, animals, things, ideas, images, ourselves. It flies in the face of social hierarchies. We toss together elements that were formerly separate. Our actions take on novel sequences. To play is to free ourselves from arbitrary restrictions and expand our field of action. Our play fosters richness of response and adaptive flexibility. This is the evolutionary value of play—play makes us flexible. By reinterpreting reality and begetting novelty, we keep from becoming rigid. Play enables us to rearrange our capacities and our very identity so that they can be used in unforeseen ways.

"Play" is different from "game." Play is the free spirit of exploration, doing and being for its own pure joy. Game is an activity defined by a set of rules, like baseball, sonnet, symphony, diplomacy. Play is an attitude, a spirit, a way of doing things, whereas game is a defined activity with rules and a playing field and participants. It is possible to engage in games like baseball or the composing of fugues as play; it is also possible to experience them as *lîla* (divine play), or as drudgery, as bids for social prestige, or even as revenge.

Acts are pulled from their normal context into the special context of play. Often we establish a protected setting or play-space, though if we feel free enough we may play even in the face of great danger. The special context is marked by the message "This is play"—a dog waggling its tail, a smile, a shine in our eyes, the doorway to a theater, the dimming of the lights in the concert hall.

Anthropologists have found "galumphing" to be one of the prime talents that characterize higher life forms.[13] Galumphing is the immaculately rambunctious and seemingly inexhaustible play-energy apparent in puppies, kittens, children, baby baboons—and also in young communities and civilizations. Galumphing is the seemingly useless elaboration and ornamentation of activity. It is profligate, excessive, exaggerated, uneconomical. We galumph when we hop instead of walk, when we take the scenic route instead of the efficient one, when we play a game whose rules demand a limitation of our powers, when we are interested in means rather than in ends. We voluntarily create obstacles in our path and then enjoy overcoming them. In the higher animals and in people, it is of supreme evolutionary value.

Galumphing ensures that we remain on the upside of the law of requisite variety. This fundamental law of nature[14] states that a system intended to handle x amount of information must be able to take on at least x different states of being. In photography, for example, if we want to capture three levels of light, we need a camera with at least three apertures or shutter speeds. In music, if we want to transmit three kinds of emotion, we need to be able to draw the bow or blow our breath or strike the keys with at least three kinds of touch—preferably many more. This is what we call "having technique to burn"—having more powerful and flexible means available to us than we need in any given situation. A would-be artist may have the most profound visions, feelings, and insights, but without skill there is no art. The requisite variety that opens up our expressive possibilities comes from practice, play, exercise, exploration, experiment. The effects of nonpractice (or of insufficiently risky practice) are rigidity of heart and body, and an ever-shrinking compass of available variety.

In play, animals, people, or whole societies get to experiment with all sorts of combinations and permutations of body forms, social forms, thought forms, images, and rules that would not be possible in a world that functions on immediate survival values. A creature that plays is more readily adaptable to changing contexts and conditions. Play as free improvisation sharpens our capacity to deal with a changing world. Humanity, playing through our prolific variety of cultural adaptations, has spread over the whole globe, survived several ice ages, and created stupendous artifacts.

We are taught (by the Book of Ecclesiastes and the second law of thermodynamics) that the world of matter and energy falls in the natural course of things from order into disorder. But life reveals the inherent countercurrent to this tendency, transforming matter and energy into more and more organized patterns through the ongoing game of evolution. This proliferation of variety seems to be self-energizing, self-motivating, and self-enriching, like play itself.

There is a German word, *funktionslust,* which means the pleasure of doing, of producing an effect, as distinct from the pleasure of attaining the effect or having something. Creativity exists in the searching even more than in the finding or being found. We take pleasure in energetic repetition, practice, ritual. As play, the act is its own destination. The focus is on process, not product. Play is intrinsically satisfying. It is not conditioned on anything else. Play, creativity, art, spontaneity, all these experiences are their own rewards and are blocked when we perform for reward or punishment, profit or loss. For this reason, "Man cannot live by bread alone."[15]

Play is without "why." It is self-existent: We are reminded of the conversation between Moses and God in Exodus: Moses wants to know what to tell the people when they ask who he's been talking to, who gave the inspiration. God simply says, "I am that I am." Play is done that it is done.

Like *lîla,* or divine creativity, art is a gift, coming from a place of joy, self-discovery, inner knowing. Play, intrinsically rewarding, doesn't cost anything; as soon as you put a price on it, it becomes, to some extent, not play. Somewhere, therefore, we each have to map for ourselves the tricky questions of money and the artist. This is a difficult issue because artists have to eat, equip themselves, and subsidize years of professional training. Yet the marketplace shifts our art at least to some degree out of the state of free play, and may in some cases contaminate it totally. Professional athletes face the same issues. Certainly they play to a great extent for love of their sport, but issues of money, prestige, and fame introduce a lot of nonplay as well.

In the same way, writing is art only when you adore language itself, when you revel in the play of imagination, not when you regard it as a mere instrumentality for conveying your ideas. The purpose of literary writing is not to "make a point"; it is to provoke imaginative states. These things exist on a continuum, of course; journalism and literature are not cut-and-dried categories, nor are commercial art and expressive or visionary art.

In the myth of the flute player, when he plays for approval, plays for prestige, plays to meet the expectations of his teacher or to avoid shame, there is always something lacking. But when he has nothing to gain and nothing to lose, then he can really *play*.

In the realm of myths and symbols, the spirit of play is represented by a number of archetypes: the Fool, the Trickster, the Child. The Fool is an ancient tarot image in our culture, number zero in the deck, representing pure potentiality. Sacred clowns and fools appear in the mythologies and traditional poesies of civilizations worldwide, in such figures as the American Indian gods Trickster and Coyote, the Greek Pan, and the clowns and fools of Renaissance Italy, England, and France. The wisdom of the fool is a theme that flows throughout Shakespeare's work. Fools, tricksters, holy buffoons, and also shamans to some degree, served in a way as muses, channeling the straight talk of the unconscious without the fear or shame that inhibits normal adults. Trickster is untamed, unpredictable, innocent, sometimes destructive, arising from pre-Creation times, galumphing through life unmindful of past or future, good or evil. Always improvising, unmindful of the consequences of his acts, he may be dangerous; his own experiments often blow up in his face or in others'. But because his play is completely free and untrammeled ("For fools rush in where angels fear to tread"[16]) he is the creator of culture and, in many myths, the creator of the other gods. He calls all the objects in the world younger

THE FOOL .

brothers, speaking the language of every one of them.[17] Trickster is one of our guardian spirits, keeping alive the childhood of humanity.

The most potent muse of all is our own inner child. The poet, musician, artist continues throughout life to contact this child, the self who still knows how to play. "Whosoever," said Jesus, "does not receive the Kingdom of God as a little child shall not enter into it."[18] Improvisation, as playful experiment, is the recovery in each of us of the savage mind, our original child-mind. Psychoanalysts sometimes speak of this recovery as "regression in the service of the ego."[19] But it's not in the service of the ego, it's in the service of the total Self.

Full-blown artistic creativity takes place when a trained and skilled grown-up is able to tap the source of clear, unbroken play-consciousness of the small child within. This consciousness has a particular feel and flow we instinctively recognize. It is "like tossing a ball on swift-flowing water: moment-to-moment nonstop flow."[20]

A girl riding her bike discovers that the secret of effortless control is balance—continuous adjustment of continuous

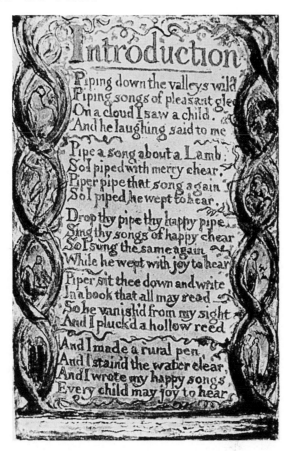

Introduction

Piping down the valleys wild
Piping songs of pleasant glee
On a cloud I saw a child.
And he laughing said to me

Pipe a song about a Lamb;
So I piped with merry chear,
Piper pipe that song again
So I piped he wept to hear.

Drop thy pipe thy happy pipe
Sing thy songs of happy chear
So I sung the same again
While he wept with joy to hear

Piper sit thee down and write
In a book that all may read
So he vanish'd from my sight
And I pluck'd a hollow reed

And I made a rural pen,
And I staind the water clear,
And I wrote my happy songs
Every child may joy to hear

change. When she reaches the point of shouting, "Look, Ma, no hands!" she has learned that she can use less and less means to control greater and greater power. She has learned to encounter and consciously play with rhythm, timing, weight, balance, geometry, right- and left-handed coordination. She does this by herself, from her own body. The emotions attendant on such a discovery are fear, delight, pride, disbelief, elation, and a desire to try it again and again.

This is what classically trained musicians feel when they discover that they can play without a score. It is like throwing down a crutch. It may seem somewhat crude to refer to the likes of Beethoven and Bach, who have always sat on the right hand of God, as a crutch. But what we learn from our newly improvising body is that it can be debilitating to depend on the creativity of others. When this creative power that depends on no one else is aroused, there is a release of energy, simplicity, enthusiasm. The word *enthusiasm* is Greek for "filled with *theos*"—filled with God.

When our flute master comes to town, he plays something utterly simple. He has the technique to burn, he can play anything, but he plays something simple, and it is incredibly powerful, godlike play. His student, after years of suffering, finally plays in the same way. The work may hold a lot of tension, a lot of soul, but it is utterly simple.

As we will see in the chapters that follow, it can sometimes be a heartbreaking struggle for us to arrive at a place where we are no longer afraid of the child inside us. We often fear that people won't take us seriously, or that they won't think us qualified enough. For the sake of being accepted, we can forget our source and put on one of the rigid masks of professionalism or conformity that society is continually offering us. The childlike part of us is the part that, like the Fool, simply does and says, without needing to qualify himself or strut his credentials.

Like other manifestations of the Muse, the child is the voice of our own inner knowing. The first language of this knowing is play. In this light, psychiatrist Donald Winnicott came to clarify the aim of psychological healing as "bringing the patient from a state of not being able to play into a state of being able to play. . . . It is in playing and only in playing that the individual child or adult is able to be creative and to use the whole personality, and it is only in being creative that the individual discovers the self."[21]

Disappearing

*Inspiration may be a form of superconsciousness,
or perhaps of subconsciousness—I wouldn't know.
But I am sure that it is the antithesis of self-
consciousness.*

AARON COPLAND

For art to appear, we have to *disappear*. This may
sound strange, but in fact it is a common experience. The
elementary case, for most people, is when our eye or ear is
"caught" by something: a tree, a rock, a cloud, a beautiful
person, a baby's gurgling, spatters of sunlight reflected off
some wet mud in the forest, the sound of a guitar wafting
unexpectedly out of a window. Mind and sense are arrested
for a moment, fully in the experience. Nothing else exists.
When we "disappear" in this way, everything around us
becomes a surprise, new and fresh. Self and environment
unite. Attention and intention fuse. We see things just as we
and they are, yet we are able to guide and direct them to
become just the way we want them. This lively and vigorous
state of mind is the most favorable to the germination of
original work of any kind. It has its roots in child's play, and
its ultimate flowering in full-blown artistic creativity.

We have all observed the intense absorption of children
in play, that wide-eyed concentration in which both the child
and the world vanish, and there is only the play. Grown-ups
involved in work they love also can experience such moments. It is possible to *become* what you are doing; these times
come when pouf!—out you go, and there is only the work.
The intensity of your focused concentration and involvement
maintains and augments itself, your physical needs decrease,

your gaze narrows, your sense of time stops. You feel alert and alive; effort becomes effortless. You lose yourself in your own voice, in the handling of your tools, in your feeling for the rules. Absorbed in the pure fascination of the game, of the textures and resistances and nuances and limitations of that particular medium, you forget time and place and who you are. The noun of self becomes a verb. This flashpoint of creation in the present moment is where work and play merge.

Buddhists call this state of absorbed, selfless, absolute concentration *samadhi*. *Samadhi* is best known to be attainable through the practice of meditation, though there is also walking *samadhi*, cooking *samadhi*, sandcastle-building *samadhi*, writing *samadhi*, fighting *samadhi*, lovemaking *samadhi*, flute-playing *samadhi*. When the self-clinging personality somehow drops away, we are both entranced and alert at the same time.

Babies of our own and other species seem to be often, if not usually, in a state of *samadhi*, and also have the unique property of putting everyone around them into a state of *samadhi* as well. Happy, relaxed, unmindful of self, concentrated, the baby envelops us in her own state of divine delight and expansiveness. Even when a baby is squalling and miserable, and making everyone else miserable too, she is whole and thorough about it, and is generating her own special atmosphere of squalling *samadhi* and misery-making *samadhi*.

The Sufis call this state *fanà*, the annihilation of the individual selfhood. In *fanà*, the characteristics of the little self dissolve so that the big Self can show through. Because of this transpersonal grounding, artists, though they use the idioms of their own place and time, are able to speak personally to each one of us even across considerable gaps of time, space, and culture.

The Sufis also speak of a related experience, *samä*, which means dancing yourself into ecstasy. In this state, body and

mind are so intensely occupied with activity, the brain waves
are so thoroughly entrained by the compelling and powerful
rhythms, that ordinary self is left behind and a form of
heightened awareness arises. Rumi, the great Persian poet
and choreographer (it was he who originated the whirling
dervishes), wrote:

> *Dancing is not getting up painlessly like a speck of*
> *dust blown around in the wind.*
> *Dancing is when you rise above both worlds, tearing*
> *your heart to pieces, and giving up your soul.*
> *Dance where you can break yourself to pieces and totally*
> *abandon your worldly passions.*
> *Real men dance and whirl on the battlefield; they dance*
> *in their own blood.*
> *When they give themselves up, they clap their hands;*
> *When they leave behind the imperfections of the self,*
> *they dance.*
> *Their minstrels play music from within; and whole*
> *oceans of passion foam on the crest of the waves.*[22]

It is curious that both meditation and dancing are ways
to "disappear." The world's cultures are full of very specific
and technical means for getting to this state of emptiness.
Whether Apollonian in character, like Zen, or Dionysian in
character, like Sufism, these traditions and the practices they
prescribe take us out of ordinary time. Slowing body/mind
activity down to nothing, as in meditation, or involving us in
a highly skilled and exhausting activity, as in dancing or
playing a Bach partita, the ordinary boundaries of our identity disappear, and ordinary clock-time stops.

Keith Johnstone, who left the directorship of one of the
big London theaters to found the Loose Moose Improvisational Theatre in Calgary, invented this exercise for bringing
a group of ten or twenty actors into *samadhi:* (1) Everyone

keep eyes popped open and round, as big as possible; (2) Everyone (on signal) march around the room and point at any and every object and shout as loudly as possible the wrong name for it (call a rug a bus, call a chandelier a dog, and so on); (3) Go! Fifteen to twenty seconds of this chaos is plenty. Suddenly everything looks as fresh as can be; all our habitual overlays of interpretation and conceptualization are removed from the objects and people in front of us. This is very much like what people report of psychedelic states induced by drugs, a very pure awareness of things-in-themselves; but it is much less costly to the physiology.

The meditative techniques for dipping into *samadhi* are many, and they come from all over the world. Here is one, just for flavor. Breathe deeply, nostrils open, eyes half-open. Breathe from the bottom of the belly only; squeeze the air out, then relax to let the air in. Squeeze, relax; let the cycles become slower and slower, until the breaths become a steady wave like the calm ocean. Mouth closed, tongue on the roof of the mouth, spine as long as it can possibly get, shoulders dropped low. The longer the meditation, the longer and easier the spine gets, relaxed and alert. Let belly breath become whole-body breath. Let spine stretch up to the zenith and down into the earth: a tree whose roots are infinitely deep and whose branches are beyond the clouds. Circulate the light. As belly relaxes and air flows in, let the light circulate upward, from the root of spine all the way up through the brain. As air squeezes out, let the light flow down the front of the body, through chest and arms, stomach, legs, and gather once again in a coil at the root of the spine. Let the minutes pass. When you finally stand up, recover your own body, in which the light continues to circulate of its own accord.

Then, slowly, pick up the tools of your art, test their weight and balance, and make the first strokes.

One of the great ways of emptying the self, along with

meditation, dance, love, and play, is tuning a musical instrument. In tuning an instrument we are forced to obliterate outside noises and distractions: As the sound gets closer and closer to the pure vibration we are trying for, as the pitch moves up and down over a smaller and smaller range, we find body and mind progressively dropping away. We enter more and more deeply into the sound. We enter into a kind of trance state. This intensified listening is *deep play*—total immersion in the game. And once we pick up that instrument to play, our friends the audience will enter into a similar state of mind more readily in proportion to the care we have given to that process of tuning. What we discover, mysteriously, is that in tuning the instrument we tune the spirit.

An even simpler *samadhi* exercise is this: Look at whatever is in front of you and say, "Yes! Yes! Yes!" to it, like Molly Bloom's life-affirming, love-affirming mantra at the end of *Ulysses.* The universe of possibilities becomes visibly, tangibly larger, over a period of mere moments. When you say, "No, No, No," the world gets smaller and heavier. Try it both ways and verify the truth of this very simple method. Look at water lilies or other highly vascular flowering plants. When the sun comes out, the flowers unfold before your eyes; when the sun goes away, they close. What the sun's radiation and the lilies say to each other, translated through the biophysical language of chlorophyll, sugar, protein, and water, is, "Yes! Yes! Yes!"

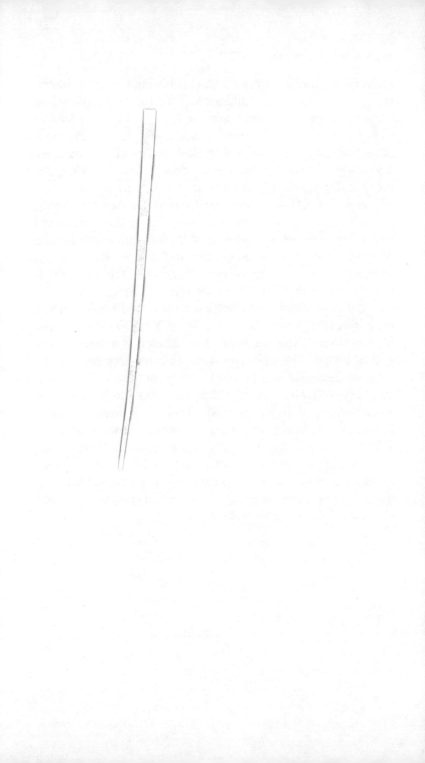

The Work

Sex and Violins

I am always between two currents of thought: first the material difficulties, turning round and round and round to make a living; and second, the study of color. I am always hoping to make a discovery here, to express the feelings of two lovers by a marriage of two complementary colors, their mingling and their opposition, the mysterious vibrations of kindred tones. To express the thought behind a brow by the radiance of a bright tone against a somber background. To express hope by some star, the eagerness of a soul by a sunset glow.

VINCENT VAN GOGH

I want to describe here a little of what it feels like to play the violin, what some of the physical and spiritual moves are. Each art has its own moves, and its own fields of play. Just as van Gogh in handling paint dealt as his daily, practical work with such things as color, radiance, vibration, hope, eagerness, and a somber background, so does each of us. Whatever means of expression we have chosen or received has its own feel. This is the integration, in practice, of inspiration, the muse, play, the vehicle, the stream—all of our sources.

Music has always served as relief and medicine for the pressures of life, but it is also a strengthening exercise, for both listener and player. Playing a string instrument in particular provides the entire body and mind with a thorough and demanding workout. The energetic impulse that moves the bow surges up from the earth through the feet and hips into the shoulder and down the nerves and muscles of the right arm. The informational impulse comes from past, present,

59

and future, through the body, brain, and personality to descend, again, down the nerves and muscles of the arms and hands, right through the instrument.

Here is William Blake's prayer to the Muses who bring him his poetry and painting:

> *Come into my hand*
> *By your mild power; descending down the Nerves of my right*
>   *arm*
> *From out the Portals of my Brain, where by your ministry*
> *The Eternal Great Humanity Divine planted his Paradise.*[23]

The violinist's right arm drawing the bow creates time: quantities of time in the rhythms and tempos at which the bow rubs the strings, as well as qualities of time in the differences of touch, balance, and strength given to different parts within a single tone, playing the rhythms roughly or gently, staccato or legato. The bow may run, slip, slither over the strings; it may bounce, scratch, caress, gush, pound, attack, whisper. Each inch of the bow from top to bottom has its own character, its own qualities of weight, tension, fluid dynamics, which it imparts to the sound.

Meanwhile, the left hand is creating space. To the bow's male, the violin is female, creating and controlling the ever-changing size and shape of the vibrational space. The thumb supports the violin in a dynamic state of balance, while the fingers stop the strings to change their vibrating length. A thick or long string creates a deep, fat sound; a short or thin string creates a high, piercing sound. And as in bowing, the fingers stopping the string create not only the size of the vibrational space (pitch) but also its shape and color, coming down on the string with a hard slap or a soft squeeze, with vibrato gentle or frenetic, to create a whole universe of emotional character within a single note.

There is, in fact, no such thing as a "note" in music. A

note is an abstract symbol representing a tone, which is an actual sound. You can play thousands of so-called B's or C's and they will all be different. Nothing can be standardized. Each vibratory event is unique.

There are four levels of vibration coexistent in music. The middle levels, which are the ones explicitly described in notation, are pitch and rhythm. Vibrations between twenty and several thousand cycles per second are experienced as tones with discernible pitch. As the frequency falls below twenty or so (you can verify this by listening to the bottom tones of a piano or tuba, or by gradually turning down the throttle on a motor), the waves seem to our ears to break up into discrete chunks of sound, and we experience not pitch but rhythm. In ordinary music we hear several layers (harmonies) of fast tonal waves, superimposed with slower rhythm waves. At the micro level underneath these layers of waves are waves of subtle vibration that modify and vary the pitch and the rhythm—these are the vibratos, the rubatos, the hesitations and surgings within each tone, which constitute the personal expressiveness of the individual player. Then at the macro level inclusive of the others are the very big, slow waves of change that constitute the overall form and structure of the piece, its dynamic flow of pattern from beginning to end.

The violin is a ruthlessly honest seismograph of the heart. Four strings stretched over the bridge put sixty-five pounds of pressure on the wooden sounding chamber; this stored energy amplifies every nuance of weight, balance, friction, and muscle tone as the musician draws the bow over the string. Each tremor and movement reflects the musician's minutest unconscious impulse. There is nothing hidden with the violin—it is like mathematics in that respect; pretense is impossible. The sound coming out of that instrument is a sensitive lie detector, a sensitive truth detector.

Playing is entirely empirical, testing its own mettle in

real time. It is not a matter of theory or learning the right way to play, but of doing by doing and discovery by experiment.

As everyone who has tried playing a violin knows, the biggest problem is playing in tune. The strings have no frets or other guideposts on them to tell you where to put your fingers (sometimes we see children's violins defaced by sticking little pieces of Scotch tape on the fingerboard as markers for the so-called notes, but this beastliness only makes things worse).

With intonation, as with every other aspect of violin playing, there is nothing to be taken for granted. Especially in the big jumps of the hand between the lowest and highest positions, it seems to be a matter of aiming and shooting at an unmarked target. Very risky. And way up there in the upper registers, if the finger is off by a fraction the sound can be quite disturbing. As a child—having been far from a prodigy—I thought that playing in perfect tune was a matter of making a lucky shot (as in pin-the-tail-on-the-donkey) and that playing up high on that E-string the world's most death-defying high-wire act.

I eventually discovered that the violinist never makes those jumps at a single shot, but continuously adjusts the sound's pitch by ear, at lightning speed. The finger doesn't come down on the spot and stay there; it glides up and down by minute intervals, microtonally, until it matches what the ear wants to hear. When we are flexible and sensitive, we are always sliding into base in a continuous dance of feedback, just as an athlete is always dancing around in order to meet the ball at the precise time and place.

Our muscles can't do this unless the fingers are soft and relaxed. If we use just enough force to press the string, it's easy to nudge the finger up and down smoothly in tenths of a second. But if more than just enough force is used (human hands are very strong!), the finger will be temporarily glued to where it landed, and presto—you have an audible mistake.

In the science of psychophysics there is a law (the Weber-Fechner law) that relates the objective value of stimulation (a light, a sound, a touch) to its subjective value (the sensation we feel). The gist of it is that our sensitivity diminishes in proportion to the total amount of stimulation. If there are two candles lit in a room, we easily notice the difference in brightness when a third candle is lit. But if there are fifty candles burning, we are unlikely to notice the difference made by a fifty-first. If there is less total stimulation, each small change makes more of a difference, or in Gregory Bateson's phrase, it's a difference that makes a difference. Against a background that is quiet and stress-free, subtle sounds and movements can have a very dramatic effect.

That is why the best form of ear-cleaning is to spend a month in the country, away from loud machine noises, crowds, and traffic. Each day, as the ear gradually recovers some of its primeval power, we begin to hear more and more. The same is true of the kinesthetic sense. The harder we press on a violin string, the less we can feel it. The louder we play, the less we hear. The more relaxed and ready the muscles are, the more different ways they can move. The method is to free up the hands, arms, shoulders, every part of the body, making them strong, soft, and supple so that inspiration can pass unimpeded down the nerve-muscle-mind channels. Unimpeded by what? By involuntary contractions of the voluntary muscles, by spasms of will. Our fears, doubts, and rigidities are manifested physiologically, as excessive muscular tension, or what Wilhelm Reich called "body armor." If I "try" to play, I fail; if I force the play, I crush it; if I race, I trip. Any time I stiffen or brace myself against some error or problem, the very act of bracing would cause the problem to occur. The only road to strength is vulnerability.

One year I decided to relearn to play the violin from scratch, unlearning everything I had learned before, while living in a house shared with friends. Practicing an instrument can be a great disturbance! I had to learn to play so softly that my music could barely be heard a few inches away, and yet play with a tone that was interesting enough to keep me playing. I learned to barely tickle the strings so that they just whispered, yet whispered clearly and easily.

I was also particularly fortunate then (though I did not think so at the time!) to be suffering from a painful neck injury that took several months to heal. Grasping the instrument with my head was out of the question. I had to keep the violin suspended in midair using only the smallest muscular contractions, a light, dynamic impulse of support that traveled up and down the nerves of my left arm without ever binding or clinging in any one spot. This experience taught me weightlessness and the achievement of ease.

I found myself paying minute attention to what happens

to the muscle groups as I played: how they developed; how they strengthened; how good the fatigue felt; how the more I played in different ways, the more I relaxed and strengthened the whole body. Playing the instrument means finding the graceful, balanced form for each action, so that weight is distributed and muscles hold no excessive tensions.

How do the muscle groups interact for a pianist? For a potter? For a photographer? For a basketball center?

I found that concentrating on body, gravity, balance, technique—the physicality of the instrument—left room for inspiration to sneak in unimpeded. From this empty space came all my subsequent adventures in improvisation.

The 150 taut bow hairs, ever moving, are an extension of the player's right arm; they are an extension of brain; they are an extension of bloodstream. Right and left hands make a matched pair that, like male and female, is both symmetrical and complementary. Right and left, violin and bow, male and female, music and silence; the couples dance, combine, struggle, mingle, merge, separate. This sexual polarity is an authentic experience regardless of whether the violinist is personally male or female. Both men and women have male and female sides to their personalities, animus and anima. Often we function by repressing one side or the other. But to play the violin and bow freely together, the violinist has to have both sides operating easily and openly. The violin has her own past, present, and future; the bow has his own past, present, and future. Only in their comingling is music generated. One hand clapping is no-sound. Music takes two. If there is a clash or misunderstanding, if right and left hand forget each other, the best way to get them back into love is to re-enter that subtle awareness that is attained by playing very, very softly, and listening.

That is why it is so wonderful to fiddle at 3 A.M. without disturbing the neighbors.

Practice

The very act of putting my work on paper, of, as we say, kneading the dough, is for me inseparable from the pleasure of creation. So far as I am concerned, I cannot separate the spiritual effort from the psychological and physical effort; they confront me on the same level and do not present a hierarchy.

IGOR STRAVINSKY

Unless you have been thoroughly drenched in perspiration you cannot expect to see a palace of pearls on a blade of grass.

THE BLUE CLIFF RECORD

Anyone who studies an instrument, sport, or other art form must deal with practice, experiment, and training. We learn only by doing. There is a gigantic difference between the projects we imagine doing or plan to do and the ones we actually do. It is like the difference between a fantasied romance and one in which we really encounter another human being with all his or her complexities. Everyone knows this, yet we are inevitably taken aback by the effort and patience needed in the realization. A person may have great creative proclivities, glorious inspirations, and exalted feelings, but there is no creativity unless creations actually come into existence.

Conservatories and music departments have long corridors lined with rows of tiny practice rooms, each containing a piano and a music stand, with walls more or less sound-proofed. Once I was walking down such a corridor when I came upon a room that had just been converted into an office. A sign was taped on the door: THIS IS NO LONGER A PRAC-

TICE ROOM. Some trickster had come along later and scribbled underneath: NOW IT'S PERFECT!

Our stereotypical formula, "practice makes perfect," carries with it some subtle and serious problems. We think of practice as an activity done in a special context to prepare for performance or the "real thing." But if we split practice from the real thing, neither one of them will be very real. Through this split, many children have been irrevocably taught to hate the piano or violin or music itself by the pedantic drill of oppressively boring exercises. Many others have been taught to hate literature, mathematics, or the very idea of productive work.

The most frustrating, agonizing part of creative work, and the one we grapple with every day in practice, is our encounter with the gap between what we feel and what we can express. "Something lacking," said the flute player's master. Often we look at ourselves and feel that *everything* is lacking! It is in this gap, this zone of the unknown, where we feel most deeply—but are most inarticulate.

Technique can bridge this gap. It also can widen it. When we see technique or skill as a "something" to be attained, we again fall into the dichotomy between "practice" and "perfect," which leads us into any number of vicious circles. If we improvise with an instrument, tool, or idea that we know well, we have the solid technique for expressing ourselves. But the technique can get too solid— we can become so used to knowing how it should be done that we become distanced from the freshness of today's situation. This is the danger that inheres in the very competence that we acquire in practice. Competence that loses a sense of its roots in the playful spirit becomes ensconced in rigid forms of professionalism.

The Western idea of practice is to acquire a skill. It is very much related to our work ethic, which enjoins us to endure struggle or boredom now in return for future rewards. The Eastern idea of practice, on the other hand, is to create the person, or rather to actualize or reveal the complete person who is already there. This is not practice *for* something, but complete practice, which suffices unto itself. In Zen training they speak of sweeping the floor, or eating, as practice. Walking as practice.

When we explode the artificial categories of *exercise* and *real music,* each tone we play is at once an exploration of technique and a full expression of spirit. No matter how expert we may become, we need to continually relearn how to play with beginner's bow, beginner's breath, beginner's body. Thus we recover the innocence, the curiosity, the desire that impelled us to play in the first place. Thus we discover the necessary unity of practice and performance. It was this tasty sense of process that first clued me in to the practical relevance of Zen to music.

Not only is practice necessary to art, it *is* art.

You don't have to practice boring exercises, but you do have to practice something. If you find the practice boring, don't run away from it, but don't tolerate it either. Transform it into something that suits you. If you are bored playing a scale, play the same eight tones but change the order. Then change the rhythm. Then change the tone color. Presto, you have just improvised. If you don't think the result is very good, you have the power to change it—now there is both a supply of raw material and some judgment to feed back into the process. This is especially effective with classically trained musicians who think they can't play without a score, or can't develop technique without exact repetition of some exercise in a book. But it also applies to the scales of dance, drawing, theater. In any art we can take the most basic and simple technique, shift it around and personalize it until it becomes something that engages us.

Exercise of technique is not boring or interesting in and

of itself; it is we who manufacture the boredom. "Boredom," "fascination," "play," "drudgery," "high drama," "seduction"—all are names of contexts that we place on what we do and how we perceive it.

Improvisation is not "just anything"; it can have the same satisfying sense of structure and wholeness as a planned composition. But there is a case to be made for the opposite side. There is a time to do just anything, to experiment without fear of consequences, to have a play space safe from fear of criticism, so that we can bring out our unconscious material without censoring it first. One such sphere is therapy, in which we enjoy perfect confidentiality that enables us to explore the deepest and most troubling matters in our lives. Another is the art studio, where we can try things and throw them away, as many times as necessary. Brahms once remarked that the mark of an artist is how much he throws away. Nature, the great creator, is always throwing things away. A frog lays several million eggs at a sitting. Only a few dozen of these become tadpoles, and only a few of those become frogs. We can let imagination and practice be as profligate as nature.

It is well known that one can jump-start the creative process by automatic writing, just letting words flow without censoring them or judging them. One can always throw them in the trash later. No one needs to know.

The social form of automatic writing is brainstorming, in which a group of people sit together and blast out ideas without fear of shame or foolishness. The therapeutic form is free association, drilling down into preconscious and unconscious material and letting it emerge in a free-form way. In the visual arts there is automatic drawing—let's call it handstorming.

If you are a touch typist and have a computer, close your eyes and type. Just let the words go from heart to fingertips.

Don't let eyes or brain get into it at all. You can go back later and have the computer check the typos. If you do not type by touch and do not have a computer, if you paint or sail or carve wood, invent your own way of doing this. Just invent some channel of flow from heart to reality and a way of recording it so that at a later time, in another mood, you can judge the work and correct it. Practice this totally judgment-free, discrimination-free pouring out of heart. Then, maybe months or minutes later—and this is where your art form comes to resemble musical improvisation—begin to merge the mode of free play and the mode of judgment into the same moment. Slowly open your eyes as you write, let your knowledge of language and literature, culture and craftsmanship, filter into the pouring of heart onto paper, heart onto computer screen, heart onto wood.

I like the feeling in my fingers when I have been playing the keyboard on which I write this book. There is an increasing ease as I move my hands over the keys, playing with the pure kinesthetic feel of moving my hands, touching, marking, releasing in rhythm. I can cultivate this feeling whether the medium I am handling is a computer keyboard or a yellow pad or some napkins I scribble on in a restaurant.

In automatic writing and other forms of free experimentation we allow ourselves to say anything, no matter how outrageous, no matter how idiotic, because the childish, repetitive, singsong iteration of seeming nonsense (as in *Finnegans Wake*) is the pay dirt from which creative work is mined and refined. In practice we have a safe context in which to try not only what we can do but what we cannot yet do. Before we improvise with musical instruments on which we have some skill, we might improvise with our voices, bodies, household objects, simple percussion instruments, and explore the essence of sound. Dogs make excellent impromptu percussion instruments, and love the attention.

We can focus in on small acts. In automatic writing, the

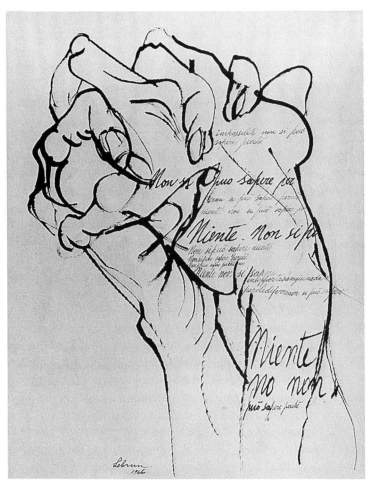

words may be nonsense, but I may focus on the clarity of handwriting, if I am writing on paper, or the accuracy of keystrokes, if writing on a keyboard. On the violin I may play any musical content at all, but focus carefully on all the ways to subtly vary finger pressure. Strangely, the nonsense often turns out to be quite beautiful precisely because I am looking elsewhere, concentrating on making one micro-aspect of technique interesting and impeccable. Making the small acts impeccable entrains body, speech, and mind into a single stream of activity. It is this physical exercise that joins the inspiration with the finished product.

For the artist this is one of the most delicate balancing acts—on the one hand, it is very dangerous to separate practice from the "real thing"; on the other hand, if we start judging what we do we will not have the safe space in which to experiment. Our practice resonates between both poles. We are "just playing," so as to be free to experiment and explore without fear of premature judgment. At the same time we play with total commitment. T. S. Eliot said that each word, each action "is a step to the block, to the fire, down the sea's throat."[24] And artist Rico Lebrun said, "I am never agitated in executing forms, but travel rather as if the terrain of the paper was land-mined. When this journey is completed, a drawing is born."[25]

Practice gives the creative processes a steady momentum, so that when imaginative surprises occur (whether they be thrown toward us by accident or brought up from within by the unconscious), they can be incorporated into the growing, breathing organism of our imagination. Here we perform the most essential synthesis—stretching out the moments of inspiration into a continuous flow of doing. Inspirations are no longer mere flashes of insight that come and go at the whim of the gods.

Thomas Edison's famous adage about inspiration and perspiration is absolutely true, but in practice there is no dualism between them; the perspiration becomes in and of itself inspiring. I come to relish solving, with my own hands, every challenge. I *meet* my material, encounter the instrument, encounter mind and body, hand and eye, encounter collaborators and audience. Practice is the entry into direct, personal, and interactive relationships. It is the linkage of inner knowing and action.

Mastery comes from practice; practice comes from playful, compulsive experimentation (the impish side of *lîla*) and from a sense of wonder (the godlike side of *lîla*). The athlete feels compelled to run around the track just one more time; the musician feels compelled to play that fugue just one more time; the potter wants to throw just one more pot before going to dinner. Then just another, please. The musician, the athlete, the dancer, move through their practice in spite of aching muscles and breathless exhaustion. This level of performance cannot be attained through some Calvinist demands of the superego, through feelings of guilt or obligation. In practice, work is play, intrinsically rewarding. It is that feeling of our inner child wanting to play for just five minutes more.

This compulsive side of practice is especially easy to experience in the new art of computer programming. The program we write is itself a responsive activity, which talks back to us in real time. We get into a loop of conversation with the program, writing and rewriting it, testing it, fixing it, testing and fixing again until we get it right, and then we find more to fix. The same applies to practicing an instrument or painting or writing. When we're really doing well and working at our peak, we show many of the signs of addiction, except it's a life-giving rather than a life-stealing addiction.

To create, we need both technique and freedom from technique. To this end we practice until our skills become unconscious. If you had to think consciously about the steps involved in riding a bicycle, you'd fall off at once. Part of the alchemy engendered by practice is a kind of cross-trading between conscious and unconscious. Technical how-to information of a deliberate and rational kind drops through long repetition from consciousness so that we can "do it in our sleep." A pianist can sometimes play Beethoven or the blues beautifully while talking about the price of fish. We can write in our native tongue without thinking at all about the laborious practice that we as children put into learning the act of making each letter.

When skill reaches a certain level, it hides itself. Many an artwork that looks simple and effortless may have been a life-and-death battlefield when the artist was creating it. When skill hides itself in the unconscious, it reveals the unconscious. Technique is the vehicle for surfacing normally unconscious material from the dream world and the myth world to where they become visible, nameable, singable.

Practice, particularly practice that involves *samadhi* states, is often characterized by ritual. Ritual is a form of galumphing, in which a special ornament or elaboration marks otherwise ordinary activity, rendering it separate and intensified, even sacred. This dawned on me one day when I was first given the opportunity to play on a Stradivarius. I simply had to wash my hands beforehand, even though they were already clean. The handwashing was a context-marker—shifting from the nine-to-five world into a sacred space defined by a beautiful and sacred implement.

I learned from such experiences, and from the trouble I have gotten myself into by ignoring them, that much of the effectiveness of practice resides in the preparation. Since practice is a repertoire of procedures we invent for ourselves, everyone's practice is different, everyone's art and craft are different. Here are a few of the preparations I have learned from my own practice. I find, paradoxically, that in preparing to create I am already creating; the *practice* and the *perfect* have already merged.

My general preparations include everything I do to be healthy and ready for surprises, with a full palette of resources available. I need energy to acquire skill, energy to practice, energy to keep going through the inevitable set-backs, energy to keep going when things look good and I am tempted to sit back and relax. I need physical energy, intellectual energy, libidinal energy, spiritual energy. The means to tapping these energies are well known: Exercise the body, eat well, sleep well, keep track of dreams, medi-tate, enjoy the pleasures of life, read and experience widely. When blocked, tap into the great block-busters: humor, friends, and nature.

The specific preparations begin when I enter the *temenos,* the play space. In ancient Greek thought, the *temenos* is a magic circle, a delimited sacred space within which special rules apply and in which extraordinary events are free to occur. My studio, or whatever space I work in, is a laboratory in which I experiment with my own consciousness. To pre-pare the *temenos*—to clear it, rearrange it, take extraneous objects out—is to clean and clear mind and body.

Even creative blocks and their resolution may be seen as one of the preparations. We will have a great deal to say about blockages later in the book, but for now, look at blocks not as a disease or anomaly, but as part of the starting proce-dure, the tuning up. I am, in the beginning, an object at rest; I have to come up against some big laws to get off that immobile place. Attempts to conquer inertia are, by defini-tion, futile. Start instead from the inertia as a focal point, develop it into a meditation, an exaggerated stillness. Let heat and momentum arise as a natural reverberation from the stillness.

When the demons of confusion and the sense of being overwhelmed strike, they can sometimes be cleared out by clearing the space. When really wrought up, try this: Clear the work table completely. Polish the surface. Get a plain, clear glass, fill it with clean water, and put it on the table. Just sit there and look at the water. Let the water be a model for stillness and clarity of mind. From clear mind, hands and body begin to move, simple and strong.

Prepare the tools. From buying the tools to cleaning and maintaining and repairing them, develop an intimate, living, years-long relationship with them. The tools need to work not only individually, but together. As I clean the room and the instruments, rearranging them, watching their relations shift, I handle elements of my life and art, moving them around, shifting their contexts. I am likely to resee the implements to my practice in new ways that may unstick my outmoded or tired ideas.

Say good-bye to distractions. Let the session flow through its three natural phases: invocation . . . work . . . thanks.

The opening ritual, taking the violin out of the case, setting up the computer, getting into the dance clothes, opening the books, mixing the paints, is pleasurable in and of itself. Having taken the instrument out of the case, explore it, feel it: How am I holding it? I tune up, including tuning the instruments, tuning the body, tuning attention, exploring and subtly balancing the feeling of bones, muscles, blood.

When I give a live performance, the stage and the whole theater become the *temenos.* The stage has to be made clean, the wiring hidden, the instruments arranged for easy use and beauty, the lighting adjusted, the ventilation made comfortable. Then I retreat and do a little meditation, a little invocation. Then I walk out on stage and begin. If at that point something is missing, I make do without it.

I eventually learned to treat each solitary writing session at home the same way I treat a live performance. In other words, I learned to treat myself with the same care and respect I give to an audience. This was not a trivial lesson.

These rituals and preparations function to discharge and clear obscurations and nervous doubts, to invoke our muses however we may conceive them, to open our capacities of mediumship and concentration, and to stabilize our person for the challenges ahead. In this intensified, turned-on, tuned-up state, creativity becomes everything we do and perceive.

The Power of Limits

*New organs of perception come into being as a result
   of necessity.
Therefore, O man, increase your necessity, so that
   you may increase your perception.*
                                    JALLALUDIN RUMI

The first great works of art we know, the paleo-
lithic cave paintings at Altamira and Lascaux, made brilliant
use of the three-dimensional surfaces that were the givens of
the creative situation. The positioning and attitudes of the
animals were suggested, even necessitated, by the bulges,
folds, crevices, and jagged textures of the rock walls on
which they were made. Some of the power of these paintings
resides in the way the painters were able to create a mutual
adaptation between the shapes of their spiritual imagination
and the shapes of hard rock.

In his enchanting novel, *A High Wind in Jamaica,* Richard Hughes describes a group of children who have been
kidnapped by pirates on the high seas and are stowed away
in the ship's cabin. One little girl is lying there, staring at the
wood grain of the plank wall next to her. She sees all sorts
of shapes and faces in the grain, and starts outlining them in
pencil. A whole fantastic scene appears.

We've all done this kind of doodling: projecting shapes
onto something, then fixing and cleaning up the outlines so
that the raw material comes to really look like what we
imagine it to be. Thus we make our inner fantasies objective
and real.

When the child completes the gestalt of the wood grain,
there is an encounter between the patterns given by the

78

seemingly random swirls of wood grain residing outside the child and the patterns given by the child's inner nature. The wood grain (or tree, or rock, or cloud) *educes,* or draws out of the child, something related to what the child knows, but that is also more or different than what the child knows because the child is both *assimilating* the outside pattern to her desires and *accommodating* herself to the outside pattern.[26] This is the eternal dialogue between making and sensing.

Here we can see why in the process of making artwork we are able to generate such sheer surprises. The artist has his training, his style, habits, personality, which might be very graceful and interesting but are nevertheless somewhat set and predictable. When, however, he has to match the patterning outside him with the patterning he brings within his own organism, the crossing or marriage of the two patterns results in something never before seen, which is nevertheless a natural outgrowth of the artist's original nature. A moiré, a crossing or marriage of two patterns, becomes a third pattern that has a life of its own. Even simple moirés made from straight lines look alive, like fingerprints or tiger stripes.

In the *I Ching,* limitation is symbolized by the joints in the bamboo stalk, the bounds that give form to the artwork and to the life. The limits are either rules of the game to which we voluntarily accede, or circumstances beyond our control that demand an adaptation. We use the limits of the body, of the instrument, of conventional forms and of new forms that we ourselves invent, as well as the limits created by our collaborators, the audience, the place in which we play, and the resources available to us. There are the limits of failure (not enough money, not enough space, not enough receptive nourishment); there are the limits of success (not enough time, being hemmed in by one's image and by the expectations of others). You can often do better art on a low

budget than on a high one. I certainly don't recommend
poverty as a modus operandi; you need the materials to
create, and there is no evidence that being well fed or able
to enjoy life damages the creative process. But necessity
forces us to improvise with the material at hand, calling up
resourcefulness and inventiveness that might not be possible
to someone who can purchase ready-made solutions.

Artists often, if not always, find themselves working
with tricky tools and intractable materials, with their inherent
quirks, resistances, inertias, irritations. Sometimes we damn

the limits, but without them art is not possible. They provide us with something to work with and against. In practicing our craft we surrender, to a great extent, to letting the materials dictate the design. The viscosity of paint, the tensile strength and wolf tones of violin strings, the egos of actors—all these foibles and limitations can be seen as the discipline that evokes creativity. Language itself is a medium rich in hindrances and resistances, as T. S. Eliot writes:

> *Words strain,*
> *Crack and sometimes break, under the burden,*
> *Under the tension, slip, slide, perish,*
> *Decay with imprecision, will not stay in place,*
> *Will not stay still. Shrieking voices*
> *Scolding, mocking, or merely chattering,*
> *always assail them.* [27]

Paradoxically, by this very outcry of frustration at the inadequacies of limited and limiting words, he plunges us into a visceral awareness of the beauty and suppleness of language.

Even James Joyce, who vastly enlarged and rearticulated the limits of language in order to fulfill the grand designs of *Finnegans Wake,* adhered to stricter, deeper rules, the rules of the dream-time, the rules of the mythos, the rules of rhythm.

The voice of the muse comes to realization in and through the limits of the body. Look at your hand. Turn it over. Stretch it. Point it. Thump it. For a musician, of all the structures that impose their discipline on us, the most ubiquitous and marvellous is the human hand. Beginning with the fact that the hand has five digits and not six or four, the hand predisposes our work toward particular conformations because it itself has a shape. The kind of music you play on the violin or piano, the kind of painting that comes from your handling of the brush, the pottery you turn on the wheel, is intimately influenced by the shape of your hands, by the way they move, by their resistances. The structure of the hand is not (once again) "just anything"; the fingers have certain characteristic relationships, certain ranges of relative movement, certain kinds of crossing, torquing, jumping, sliding, pressing, releasing movements that guide the music to come out in a certain way. Graceful work uses those patterns and instinctively moves through them and out as we find ever-fresh combinations. The shape and size of the human hand brings powerful but subtle laws into every kind of art, craftsmanship, mechanical work, and into our ideas and feelings as well. There is a continuous dialogue between hand and instrument, hand and culture. Artwork is not thought up in consciousness and then, as a separate phase, executed by the hand. The hand surprises us, creates and solves problems on its own. Often enigmas that baffle our brains are dealt with easily, unconsciously, by the hand.

In the athletic arts of dance and theater, we see this power in and of the whole body, which is the motive, the instrument, the field, and the artwork itself.

As in the case of the body, many rules and limits are God-given in that they are inherent not in styles or social conventions but in the art medium itself: the physics of sound, of color, of gravity and movement. These natural laws become the fundamentals of each art, invariant across differences of culture and historical time.

Other rules are not built into life itself, but are the rules of forms, conventional or unconventional, that we voluntarily choose to follow. We may take on improvising within a certain scale, mode, or rhythm, or in relation to a tune we know; we may take on improvising only with certain kinds of form, painting only with triangles for a while, dancing only close to the ground, or only on trapezes. This is a kind of game the artist incessantly plays, living by a contract he makes with himself. The young Picasso opened whole new territories of art by confining himself to what could be done with variants of the color blue.

Structure ignites spontaneity. Just a touch of an arbitrary form can be introduced into an improvisation to keep it from wandering off course, or to act as a catalyst, as in the seeding of a crystal. It is not necessary that the rules dictate the form of the piece, though they may. They may simply present a definite situation that can provoke a definite, if unpredictable, reaction from the artist. Ron Fein, a superb composer-pianist with whom I have collaborated on many projects, suggested one day that we go into a recording session armed with a huge pile of magazines, art books, and other visual materials to use as "scores" for violin-and-piano improvisations. An image would provoke a mood, or its opposite. The sloping shadow of an automobile would provoke a peculiar down-turning scale that would stick with us as a motif to be tossed back and forth between piano and violin. A totally ridiculous image, like a hair-spray ad, would provoke a sublime and luscious bit of music. A magnificent painting by Matisse or Remedios Varo would provoke a totally insipid bit of music that would quickly find its way to the cutting-room floor. The happiest result came when we pulled out the street map of Los Angeles. Ron played the surface streets while I played the freeways. What resulted was a frenetic, onrushing, densely organized *presto* of surprising dimensions—in spite of the fact that L.A.'s streets are actually sluggish, chaotic, and usually approaching a state of gridlock.

One rule that I have found to be useful is that *two rules are more than enough.* If we have a rule concerning harmony and another concerning rhythm, if we have a rule concerning mood and another concerning the use of silence, we don't need any more. The unconscious has infinite repertoires of structure already; all it needs is a little external structure on which to crystallize. We can let our imaginations flow freely through the territory mapped out by a pair of rules, confident that the piece will pull together as a definite entity and not a peregrination.

Limits yield intensity. When we play in the *temenos* defined by our self-chosen rules, we find that containment of strength amplifies strength. Commitment to a set of rules (a game) frees your play to attain a profundity and vigor otherwise impossible. Igor Stravinsky writes: "The more constraints one imposes, the more one frees one's self of the chains that shackle the spirit . . . and the arbitrariness serves only to obtain precision of execution."[28]

Working within the limits of the medium forces us to change our own limits. Improvisation is not breaking with forms and limitations just to be "free," but using them as the very means of transcending ourselves. If form is mechanically applied, it may indeed result in work that is conventional, if not pedantic or stupid. But form used well can become the very vehicle of freedom, of discovering the creative surprises that liberate mind-at-play. Poet Wendell Berry writes:

> There are, it seems, two Muses: the Muse of Inspiration, who gives us inarticulate visions and desires, and the Muse of Realization, who returns again and again to say, "It is yet more difficult than you thought." This is the muse of form. . . . It may be, then, that form serves us best when it works as an obstruction to baffle us and deflect our intended course. It may be that when we no longer know what to do we have come to our real work and that when we no longer know which way to go we have begun our real journey. The mind that is not baffled is not employed. The impeded stream is the one that sings.[29]

If certain values are constrained within narrow limits, others are free to vary more strongly. Thus, for example, string quartets, solos, and other limited forms may achieve greater emotional intensity than symphonies, and black-and-white photography may achieve greater power than color. In ragas, or solo jazz play, sounds are limited to a restricted sphere, within which a gigantic range of inventiveness opens up. If you have all the colors available, you are sometimes almost too free. With one dimension constrained, play becomes freer in other dimensions.

One practice I have found effective is to toss off complete improvised pieces lasting sixty seconds or less, each with a distinct beginning, middle, and end. This is an especially effective game in group improvisation with friends. These short pieces provide a limitation on one dimension, allowing for total freedom in other dimensions. Blessedly, there is no intimidating requirement to create great art. Yet the results can be surprisingly powerful in a mere forty or fifty seconds. Anton Webern, one of the seminal composers of this century, wrote many pieces of this length; they have become models of clarity and depth for composers ever since.

In a confined play space, play may become richer and subtler. We are seldom taught to fit our output to the context and the bandwidth of the tool in our hands. Classical musicians are taught to make a big sound to fill a big concert hall; rock musicians are amplified even in small rooms as though to fill a stadium. But in a smaller room with a smaller audience, or in recording, one can play subtly, barely breathing on the strings, yielding a wider dynamic range between softest and loudest. Some public speakers will yell into the microphone as though they had to fill the hall with lung power alone. Others know that they can whisper into the microphone and let the amplifier do the work. They may emphasize a point not by getting louder, but by getting softer and more intimate, subtle, suggestive. Whispered words can be devastatingly effective. The very predicaments brought on by a limited field of play, or by frustrating circumstances, often ignite the essential surprises that we later look back on as creativity.

There is a French word, *bricolage,* which means making do with the material at hand: a *bricoleur* is a kind of jack-of-all-trades or handyman who can fix anything. In popular movies, the power of *bricolage* is symbolized by the resourceful hero who saves the world with a Swiss army knife and a couple of clever tricks. The *bricoleur* is an artist of limits.

We see *bricolage* in small children, who will incorporate anything into their play—whatever piece of stuff is lying on the ground, whatever piece of information they picked up at breakfast. Dreams and myths work in the same way; in dream-time we take whatever happened that day, bits and pieces of material and events, and transform them into the deep symbolism of our own personal mythology.

These magical acts of creation are analogous to pulling a large amount of rabbit from a small amount of hat. As in the greatest known form of magic, organic growth and evolution, the output is greater than the input. There is a net gain of information, complexity, and richness. *Bricolage* implies what mathematicians like to call "elegance," that is, such economy of statement that a single line of thought has a great many implications and outcomes. In the same vein, Beethoven, writing of his favorite composer, Handel, felt that the measure of music is "producing great results from scant means."

Beethoven crafted his own music, to an amazing extent, of nothing but scales. We generally think of scales as the most elementary or boring element of music. But in Beethoven's hands, a scale is never just a scale. It is a whole natural phenomenon unto itself, like a flight of birds or a mountain range. Each note is personal, assuming an individual weight, balance, texture, and color in relation to its fellows, such as is only possible in living organisms: context within context, ever shifting, sensual.

Antonio Stradivari made some of his most beautiful violins from a pile of broken, waterlogged oars he found on the docks in Venice one day. Like the *David* hiding inside Michelangelo's rough block of marble, or the prophets and sibyls hiding behind the emptiness of his wet, freshly prepared fresco walls, in Stradivari's imagination the form of the finished violin was tangibly present in the raw chunks of wood.

In the same way, to a child's imagination a twig is a man, a bridge, a telescope. This transmutation through creative vision is the actual, day-to-day realization of alchemy. In *bricolage,* we take the ordinary materials in our hands and turn them into new living matter—the "green gold" of the alchemists. The fulcrum of the transformation is mind-at-play, having nothing to gain and nothing to lose, working and playing around the limits and resistances of the tools we hold in our hands.

One of the illusions our flute player has to drop by the wayside is that the wonder of the master's music has to do with the new flute, or the method of playing it. It's not the flute. Sometimes we think, If only I had a great instrument—a Stradivarius, a supercomputer with great graphics, a fine, perfectly equipped sculpture studio—I could do anything with it. But an artist can take the cheapest instrument and do anything with it as well. The artistic attitude, which always involves a healthy dose of *bricolage,* frees us to see the possibilities before us; then we can take an ordinary instrument and make it extraordinary.

The Power of Mistakes

Do not fear mistakes. There are none.
MILES DAVIS

Poetry often enters through the window of irrelevance.
M. C. RICHARDS

We all know how pearls are made. When a grain of grit accidentally slips into an oyster's shell, the oyster encysts it, secreting more and more of a thick, smooth mucus that hardens in microscopic layer after layer over the foreign irritation until it becomes a perfectly smooth, round, hard, shiny thing of beauty. The oyster thereby transforms both the grit and itself into something new, transforming the intrusion of error or otherness into its system, completing the gestalt according to its own oyster nature.

If the oyster had hands, there would be no pearl. Because the oyster is forced to live with the irritation for an extended period of time, the pearl comes to be.

In school, in the workplace, in learning an art or sport, we are taught to fear, hide, or avoid mistakes. But mistakes are of incalculable value to us. There is first the value of mistakes as the raw material of learning. If we don't make mistakes, we are unlikely to make anything at all. Tom Watson, for many years the head of IBM, said, "Good judgment comes from experience. Experience comes from bad judgment." But more important, mistakes and accidents can be the irritating grains that become pearls; they present us with unforeseen opportunities, they are fresh sources of inspiration in and of themselves. We come to regard our obstacles as ornaments, as opportunities to be exploited and explored.

Seeing and using the power of mistakes does not mean that anything goes. Practice is rooted in self-correction and refinement, working toward clearer and more reliable technique. But when a mistake occurs we can treat it either as an invaluable piece of data about our technique or as a grain of sand around which we can make a pearl.

Freud illuminated the fascinating way in which slips of the tongue reveal unconscious material. The unconscious is the very bread and butter of the artist, so mistakes and slips of all kinds are to be treasured as priceless information from beyond and within.

As our craft and life develop toward greater clarity and deeper individuation, we begin to have an eye for spotting these essential accidents. We can use the mistakes we make, the accidents of fate, and even weaknesses in our own makeup that can be turned to advantage.

Often the process of our artwork is thrown onto a new track by the inherent balkiness of the world. Murphy's law states that if anything can go wrong, it will. Performers experience this daily and hourly. When dealing with instruments, tape recorders, projectors, computers, sound systems, and theater lights, there are inevitable breakdowns before a performance. A performer can become sick. A valued assistant can quit at the last minute, or lose his girlfriend and become mentally incapacitated. Often it is these very accidents that give rise to the most ingenious solutions, and sometimes to off-the-cuff creativity of the highest order.

Equipment breaks down, it is Sunday night, the stores are all closed, and the audience is arriving in an hour. You are forced to do a little *bricolage,* improvising some new and crazy contraption. Then you attain some of your best moments. Ordinary objects or trash suddenly become valuable working materials, and your perceptions of what you need and what you don't need radically shift. Among the things

I love so much about performing are those totally unforeseen, impossible calamities. In life, as in a Zen koan, we
create by shifting our perspective to the point at which interruptions are the answer. The redirection of attention involved in incorporating the accident into the flow of our
work frees us to see the interruption freshly, and find the
alchemical gold in it.

Once I was preparing for a full evening poetry performance, with multiscreen slide projections and electronic
music I had composed on tape for the occasion. But in the
course of overrehearsing during the preceding week, I
managed to give myself a case of laryngitis, and woke up the
morning of the performance with a ruined voice and a high
fever. I was ready to cancel, but in the end decided that
would be no fun. Instead I dropped my attachment to my
music and preempted the sound system for use as a P.A. I sat
in an old wicker wheelchair and croaked into a microphone.
My soft, spooky, obsessive, guttural voice, amplified, became
an instrument of qualities that totally surprised me, releasing
me to find a hitherto unsuspected depth in my own poetic
line.

A "mistake" on the violin: I have been playing some
pattern: 1, 2, 3, 6; 1, 2, 3, 6. Suddenly I make a slip and play
1, 2, 3, 7, 6. It doesn't matter to me at the time whether I've
broken a rule or not; what matters is what I do in the next
tenth of a second. I can adopt the traditional attitude, treating
what I have done as a mistake: don't do it again, hope it
doesn't happen again, and in the meantime, feel guilty. Or
I can repeat it, amplify it, develop it further until it becomes
a new pattern. Or beyond that I can drop neither the old
pattern nor the new one but discover the unforeseen context
that includes both of them.

An "accident" on the violin: I am playing outdoors at
night, in misty hills. Romantic? Yes. But also humid. The
cold and the humidity take all the poop out of the bottom

string, which suddenly slackens and goes out of tune. Out of tune with what? Out of tune with my preconceived benchmark of "in tune." Again I can take the same three approaches. I can tune it back up and pretend that nothing happened. This is what politicians call "toughing it out." I can play the flabby string as is, finding the new harmonies and textures it contains. A low, thick string, when it goes flabby, not only becomes lower in pitch, but because of the flabbiness will give to the bow's weight much more easily and will produce (if lightly touched) more breathy and resonant tones than a normal string. I can have a lot of fun down there in the viola's tonal sub-basement. Or I can detune it even further, until it comes into some new and interesting harmonic relation with the other strings (*scordatura,* a technique the old Italian violinists were fond of). Now I have, instantly, a brand-new instrument with a new and different sonic shape.

An "accident" in computer graphics: I am playing with a paint program, which enables me to create visual art on the screen and then store it on disk as data that can be called up later. I intend to call up the art I was working on yesterday, but I hit the wrong key and call up the zip code index of my mailing list. The thousands of zip codes, transformed into a single glowing screen of abstract color and pattern, turn out as a startling and beautiful scene of other-worldly microscopic life. From this serendipitous blunder evolves a technique that I use to create dozens of new artworks.

The history of science, as we well know, is liberally peppered with stories of essential discoveries seeded by mistakes and accidents: Flemming's discovery of penicillin, thanks to the dust-borne mold that contaminated his petri dish; Roentgen's discovery of X rays, thanks to the careless handling of a photographic plate. Time after time, the quirks and mishaps that one might be tempted to reject as "bad data" are often the best. Many spiritual traditions point up the vitality we gain by reseeing the value of what we may have rejected as insignificant: "The stone which the builders refused," sing the Psalms of David, "has come to be the cornerstone."[30]

The power of mistakes enables us to reframe creative blocks and turn them around. Sometimes the very sin of omission or commission for which we've been kicking ourselves may be the seed of our best work. (In Christianity they speak of this realization as *felix culpa,* the fortunate fall.) The troublesome parts of our work, the parts that are most baffling and frustrating, are in fact the growing edges. We see these opportunities the instant we drop our preconceptions and our self-importance.

Life throws at us innumerable irritations that can be mobilized for pearl making, including all the irritating people who come our way. Occasionally we are stuck with a petty tyrant who makes our life hell. Sometimes these situations, while miserable at the time, cause us to sharpen, focus, and mobilize our inner resources in the most surprising ways. We become, then, no longer victims of circumstance, but able to use circumstance as the vehicle of creativity. This is the well-known principle of Jujitsu, taking your opponent's blows and using their own energy to deflect them to your advantage. When you fall, you raise yourself by pushing against the spot where you fell.

The Vietnamese Buddhist poet-priest, Thich Nhat Hanh, devised an interesting telephone meditation. The sound of the telephone ringing, and our semiautomatic instinct to jump up and answer it, seem the very opposite of meditation. Ring and reaction bring out the essence of the choppy, nervous character of the way time is lived in our world. He says use the first ring as a reminder, in the midst of whatever you were doing, of mindfulness, a reminder of breath, and of your own center. Use the second and third rings to breathe and smile. If the caller wants to talk, he or she will wait for the fourth ring, and you will be ready. What

Thich Nhat Hanh is saying here is that mindfulness, practice, and poetry in life are not to be reserved for a time and place where everything is perfect; we can use the very instruments of society's nervous pressures on us to relieve the pressure. Even under the sound of helicopters—and this is a man who buried many children in Vietnam to the roar of helicopters and bombs—he can say, "Listen, listen; this sound brings me back to my true self."

Playing Together

It takes two to know one.
GREGORY BATESON

The beauty of playing together is meeting in the One. It is astonishing how often it happens that two musicians meet for the first time, coming perhaps from very different backgrounds and traditions, and before they have exchanged two words they begin improvising music together that demonstrates wholeness, structure, and clear communication.

I play with my partner; we listen to each other; we mirror each other; we connect with what we hear. He doesn't know where I'm going, I don't know where he's going, yet we anticipate, sense, lead, and follow each other. There is no agreed-on structure or measure, but once we have played for five seconds there is a structure, because we've started something. We open each other's minds like an infinite series of Chinese boxes. A mysterious kind of information flows back and forth, quicker than any signal we might give by sight or sound. The work comes from neither one artist nor the other, even though our own idiosyncrasies and styles, the symptoms of our original natures, still exert their natural pull. Nor does the work come from a compromise or halfway point (averages are always boring!), but from a third place that isn't necessarily like what either one of us would do individually. What comes is a revelation to both of us. There is a third, totally new style that pulls on us. It is as though we have become a group organism that has its own nature and its own way of being, from a unique and unpredictable place which is the group personality or group brain.

Early on we noted that everyday speech is a case of improvisation. More than that, it's a case of shared improvisation. You meet someone new and you create language together. There is a commerce of feeling and information back and forth, exquisitely coordinated. When conversation works, it is, again, not a matter of meeting halfway. It is a matter of developing something new to both of us.

Some jobs are too big to handle alone, or simply more fun when done with friends. Either case leads us into the fruitful and challenging field of collaboration. Artists working together play out yet another aspect of the power of limits. There is another personality and style to pull with and push against. Each collaborator brings to the work a different set of strengths and resistances. We provide both irritation and inspiration for each other—the grist for each other's pearl making.

We need to remind ourselves here of what is obviously true but not often enough said: that different personality styles have different creative styles. There is no one idea of creativity that can describe it all. Therefore, in collaborating with others we round up, as in any relationship, an enlarged self, a more versatile creativity.

This brings us back to the law of requisite variety. By crossing one identity with another we multiply the variety of the total system, and at the same time each identity serves as both a check on the other and a spur to the development of the total system. That is why sexual reproduction arose so early in the history of life on earth. Because one set of genes gets married or meshed with another somewhat different set, ambivalence, change, and therefore the full riches of evolution become possible. Otherwise, evolution would still have taken place, but it would have been colossally boring. We'd all still be protozoa and slime molds, reproducing by mitosis the same dull replication of genes over and over again.

One advantage of collaboration is that it's much easier to learn from someone else than from yourself. And inertia, which is often a major block in solitary work, hardly exists at all here: A releases B's energy, B releases A's energy. Information flows and multiplies easily. Learning becomes many-sided, a refreshing and vitalizing force.

And of course there is the incalculable power of friends, even if they are not our collaborators, as the most congenial of block-busters, through conversation, support, solace, humor, and resonance, as well as the challenge, criticism, and even opposition they offer. Here is a whole vast universe of play, not only with the close friends who love us, but also with people whom we may not know so well but who some- how appear to drop just the right piece of new information in our ears at the right time (or a reminder of what we once knew but forgot). I remember, suddenly, the small green corner record store I visited at the age of fourteen, and the English record seller who crooked his finger mischievously at me, handed me an old record of the Bach Cello Suites, and said, "By the way, have you ever heard of the great Pablo Casals?"

Then there are those extraordinary spiritual friends who may appear once or twice in a lifetime, with a deep and compassionate perception of who we are and what we can become, the friends we call teachers, who may say a few words that change our lives irrevocably. They may say some- thing as simple as, "Something lacking!"

Beyond the aesthetic surprises we can find in our own exploration of our craft, we join in community with others and respond to each other, thanks to the power of *listening, watching, sensing.* The shared reality we create brings up even more surprises than our individual work. In playing together there is real risk of cacophony, the antidote to which is discipline. But this need not be the discipline of "let's agree on a structure in advance." It is the discipline of mutual awareness, consideration, listening, willingness to be subtle. Trusting someone else can involve gigantic risks, and it leads to the even more challenging task of learning to trust yourself. Giving up some control to another person teaches us to give up some control to the unconscious.

The free interplay of musicians is just one of many possible kinds of aesthetic conversation. Intermedia collaborations enrich the lives of musicians, poets, visual artists, dancers, actors, lighting designers, filmmakers, and many others. The combinations and permutations are endless, and new technologies are making old dreams of composite or integrated art forms, such as visual music, infinitely more feasible. This is a time when the multifarious worlds of music and art are beginning to meet and blend and create whole new species. We are now seeing a renaissance of crossover art of all sorts. East meets West, popular meets classical, improvisation meets tightly scored composition, video meets digital synthesizer meets Pythagorean monochord meets Balinese trance dancer. Whole cultures can play together, contribute to each other, fertilize each other.

My friend Rachel Rosenthal developed a long-running group-improvisation project in Los Angeles in the 1960s, the Instant Theater. Not only the theatrical play itself, but the costumes, sets, and lights as well were all a collective improvisation. The spotlights moved, the actors followed, in mutual call and response, mutual trust. People speaking many languages, with many skills and of many schools, can play together and create whole and lively theater. This kind of interplay has always transpired among friends, though

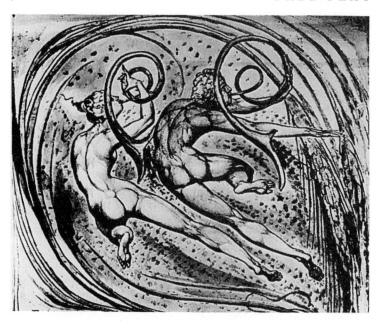

there is usually nothing concrete by which to remember the events afterward. What comes down to us (whether from last week or five centuries ago) are tantalizing rumors, like those of Leonardo da Vinci getting together with his friends at the court of Milan to present entire operas in which the music, poetry, and theatrics were made up as they went along.[31]

Artistic collaboration can run the gamut from a totally structured hierarchy, as for example a motion picture crew working from a script, to a leaderless group of performers improvising together, taking equal and shared responsibility for everything that happens.

Collective free improvisation in the performing arts, music, dance, and theater invites us into whole new kinds of human relationships and fresh harmonies, in that the

structure, idiom, and rules are not dictated by any author-
ity, but created by the players. Shared art making is, in and
of itself, the expression of, the vehicle for, and the stimulus
to human relationships. The players, in and by their play,
build their own society. As a direct relationship between
people, unmediated by anything other than their imaginations, group improvisation can be a catalyst to powerful and
unique friendships. There is an intimacy that cannot be
reached through words or deliberation, resembling in
many ways the subtle, rich, and instantaneous communication between lovers.

There is a phenomenon called entrainment, which is the
synchronization of two or more rhythmic systems into a single pulse. If a group of men is hammering on a building site,
after a few minutes they fall into the same rhythm without

any explicit communication. In the same way, the body's physiological rhythms resonate with each other; even electronic oscillators operating at close to the same frequency will entrain together. It is entrainment that provokes the trance states in the *samä* dances of the Sufis. When improvisers play together, they can rely on this natural phenomenon to mesh the music so that they breathe together, pulse together, think together.

In entrainment, the voices are not locked in exactly; they are always slightly off from each other, finding each other again and again in micromoments of time, weaving in and out of each other's rhythms. Perfect harmony can be ecstasy or an utter bore. It is the push and pull that makes it exciting.

We can play together without even playing together. For writers, art colonies or libraries are often good places to work, because even though the people around us are total strangers and are all doing their own private work, the silent rhythm of working together strengthens everyone's work energy. We feel a self-reinforcing entrainment of our concentration and commitment to *be* with our work. If one is learning meditation, to sit cross-legged for half an hour alone, silent and still, can be a difficult test of stamina. But if a group is sitting together, the physical-spiritual challenge becomes much easier to bear, and retreats of a week or more become feasible.

Entrainment mediates the performers' unity with the audience as well as with each other. A good hypnotist will tell you that you will be much more successful at putting a person into trance if you pay close attention to his or her breathing, and mold your words, their timing and tone, to the timing and tone of the breaths. This is just what one does in improvising music for audiences: learning to detect and amplify the collective breath, which, as the experience proceeds, becomes more and more synchronized, deeper. There is a quality of energy in the room that is very personal and particular to those people, that room, and that moment. As in the case of controlling autonomic body responses by bio-feedback, we don't know quite how it's done, but we know that it is done.

The separate beings of audience and performers can *disappear*, and at such moments there is a kind of secret complicity between us. We catch glances in each other's eyes and see ourselves as one. Our minds and hearts move together to the rolling of the rhythm. This is more likely to happen at informal performances where there is no stage and no fixed seating to impose a dualistic split between active performers and passive audience. Through subtle but powerful entrainments, the audience, the environment, and the players link into a self-organizing whole. Even the dogs in the room are entrained. We discover together and at the same time the rhythmic and emotional scene as it unfolds. The skin-boundaries become semipermeable, then irrelevant; performers, audience, instruments, the room, the night outside, space, become one being, pulsing.

Form Unfolding

*The body of writing takes a thousand different forms,
and there is no one right way to measure.*
*Changing, changing at the flick of a hand, its various
forms are difficult to capture.*
*Words and phrases compete with one another, but the
mind is still master.*
*Caught between the unborn & the living, the writer
struggles to maintain both depth and surface.*
*He may depart from the square, he may overstep the
circle, searching for the one true form of his reality.*
*He would fill the eyes of his readers with splendor; he
would sharpen the mind's values.*
*The one whose language is muddled cannot do it; only
when mind is clear can language be noble.*

LU CHI

How does structure arise in improvisation? How
are larger, composed art forms edited and shaped out of the
raw material of momentary inspiration? As we examine these
two related questions, we come to see free play as a self-
organizing system, questioning and answering itself about its
own identity.

Twenty Questions

P. D. Q. Bach (Peter Schickele) made a hilarious recording of Beethoven's *Fifth* accompanied by the loud-
mouthed play-by-play commentary of two dumb sportscasters.[32] The crowd is cheering the symphony on as the
sportscasters tell us how the conductor and orchestra are
scoring against each other, whether the horn player flubbed
his note, whether Beethoven is going into overtime with

102

another recap. There is some truth to this spoof. When listening to music, we subliminally ask and answer a continuous stream of questions: Where is the horn melody going? How will this modulation turn out? How will the composer get back to home base? Will this thematic development turn to the right or the left? In India's musical tradition, audiences are openly demonstrative of their active listening. They quietly cheer and chuckle during a performance as their premonitions are confirmed or surprised, or get up for a snack if it's boring, or go into deep, concentrated attention as the music reaches moments of sublimity.

Unceasingly, mind plays the old Twenty Questions game, in which one tries to guess what the other person is thinking of by asking a series of yes-or-no questions. Twenty Questions is best approached by first asking questions that cut a broad swath across unknown territory (alive or dead? male or female?), then gradually zooming in, each question refining the answers that came before. In a piece of music, the opening chord, drone, or rhythm instantly generates expectations that generate questions that in turn feed the next bit of the music. Once the musician has played something, anything at all, the next thing fits with that, or fits against it; a pattern is there to be reinforced, or modulated, or broken.

Thus, without our imposing a preconditioned intention on it, a musical improvisation can dynamically structure itself. The first selections of tones are very free, but as we continue, the selections we *have* made affect the selections we *will* make. A blank canvas or piece of paper is "without form, and void," (Genesis 1:2) but a single mark on it sets up a definite world and poses an infinite series of creative problems. In creating fiction, all we have to do is think of a bag lady and a computer salesman, and immediately a thousand questions come up, which lead to answers, which then lead to more questions, and so on.

An improvisation may run through many such cycles—

we may fold our sounds and silences down to a point of resolution, then suddenly take off again, sweeping a whole new path through time; then yet again the music resolves itself down through asking and answering questions of itself. Mistakes and accidents, or gifts of sheer inspiration, can enter at any time to fertilize the process with fresh information. The music flows on through all these changes, incorporating and assimilating them as it goes. This way of uncovering pattern in time is analogous to Michelangelo's deblocking the statue—progressively cutting away the superficial until we get a clear view of the lineaments of true self.

A musical form that illustrates this process is the reverse theme and variations, as for example in many episodes of Sibelius' symphonies, or in Keith Jarrett's powerful piano improvisation in the *Köln Concert.* In both cases, rather than state the outlines of a theme and then grow from it a series of variations, the artist begins with the most far-flung and highly ornamented elaborations on an as yet unheard-of theme. As the (reverse) development proceeds, ornaments are progressively cast off, gradually revealing the simple outlines of the theme that was hidden in there all along. We experience a shock of recognition when the fundamental motif finally bursts forth. Our feelings of aesthetic pleasure are connected, then, not only with the taste of delayed inevitability, but with this dynamic byplay or foreplay between the fundamental and the ornamental.

As questions and answers unfold, we feel the excitement of being onto something, of following a lead, as in a detective story. Among all the diverse and confusing circumstances of a fictional murder, we seek the simplifying quotient, the whodunit. Among the welter of material that comes up in an improvisation, we seek to simplify all that doodling and noodling up and down the keyboard and find the answer to the question, "What is the deep structure of theme, pattern, or emotion from which all of this arises?"

In literature, a book that has this property of self-propulsion is called a page-turner. Soap operas work in the same way. Each episode ends on a modulation, so the maximum number of questions is raised in the viewer's mind and suspended there until the next installment. At that time the pending issues receive answers that give rise to a new set of questions.

Call-and-response is one of the oldest forms of music, ritual, theater, and dance. It harkens back, perhaps, to the early mirroring interactions of mother and infant.

A major secret of aesthetics is the mobilization of this ever-moving dialogue and the delicate balance it sets up between premonitions confirmed and premonitions overturned. Any kind of form can be the container for this process. An identifiable melody, whether of the traditional tonal kind (Mozart, the Beatles) or of the more venturesome atonal kinds (Schoenberg, Coltrane) sets up a latticework of anticipation. The listener models the sound as she hears it, then compares the next piece of the melody to see how it matches and differs from the model.

Reading, listening, looking at art is a matter of active response, of dialogue with the material. Creative study entices us from one question to the next; we are bugged by the question, which generates another answer, which is itself another question. We re-create the book as we read it. As in the Twenty Questions game, we start at the edge and work our way round and round into the center. We may reread the book or rehear the music months or years later and find newer, more integrative meanings, rhythms we weren't ready to hear before, deeper music.

Similarly, great moments in science occur when the seeming complexity of the universe is suddenly resolved by seeing an underlying design or motif that explains things more deeply. One casts off hypotheses or themes, gradually zeroing in on clearer and more coherent patterns and principles. Surprises, mistakes, accidents, anomalies, and mysteries pop up to baffle us and fertilize the mind-field. These lead to new rounds of discoveries, which create the next phase of complexity, which awaits a new synthesis.

Einstein did not overthrow or invalidate Newton's laws, but rather uncovered a deeper context that encompassed both the familiar laws of mechanics and the new, strange phenomena of electromagnetism. As ideas evolve, there occurs a rhythm of systole-diastole between the rejection of mistakes and accidents, their acceptance as oddities, and their incorporation along with the old system of beliefs into a richer, more complex system.

Creation is not the replacing of nothing with something or chaos with pattern. There is no chaos; there is a vast, living world in which the rules for specifying the pattern are so complicated that after you look at a few of them you become tired. The creative act pulls out some more inclusive shape or progression that gathers an immense amount of complexity into a simple, satisfying notion.

Jokes take us through this whole cycle in a matter of seconds. The first part of the joke causes us to set up a theory about what is happening—then the punch line explosively deflates our theory and brings us to a new view. In the same way, art surprises us and shifts our frames of reference, but it also leaves us with inexorable, unresolved ambiguities. Artful composition makes surprises and shifts of direction seem inevitable to us, or makes the inevitable surprising.

These principles operate on a more extended scale in the work of a master craftsman of the novel, such as Thomas Mann. On page 3 he may give us half an image, the opening parenthesis that sets up a texture and tension of which we may not even be consciously aware. On page 283, the other half of the image appears in a much-enriched context, closing the parentheses. Only then are we aware of what he has done. These widely separated bracketings of images and ideas serve to sew together the whole fabric of the work into a metapattern. We are ready to hear the next part even though it has not sounded yet, because of the patterns that have gone before it. Each image gives the reader a preliminary, possibly preconscious pattern, which enables the novel to expand in many directions and still be whole. The art resides in giving the readers neither too much information nor too little, but the right amount to catalyze active imagination. The best art is that which does not present itself on a silver platter but rouses the reader's faculties to act.

The key to either improvising or composing is to make each moment so tantalizing that it inexorably leads us on to the next. We love to be seduced by a delayed inevitability. We love to watch the player get out onto a dangerous limb and then live the high drama of getting back from it, giving sense and shape to the whole journey. We can experience these same feelings of suspense in more traditional sonata forms chosen by the Classical and Romantic composers. The material is first stated, then elaborated, then ornamented, then turned around and then upside down (galumphing!). We have a sense of Chinese boxes opening into one another, until inevitably the final box opens up and contains—the first. Likewise, polyphonic forms like the fugues and canons of a Bartók, a Bach, or a Monteverdi are so satisfying because they involve us in a feeling of parallel universes that nevertheless merge or resolve into one.

Listen to endings in music, in prose, in film. Does the piece seem to simply stop, or does it bring about its own conclusion in its own terms? The last moment can become the ultimate flowering of the first, all the moments in between connected and interweaving. We experience a sense of satisfaction when the closure finally hits—an experience that is often accompanied by laughter, tears, or other bodily signs of being *moved*. When a piece ends well it is immediately obvious to the players and audience alike.

But our pieces do not have to contain the same qualities as a fugue, theme and variations, sonata, rondo, or any other established form in order to be successful. There are millions of ways of composing and structuring artwork. Each piece, whether improvised or written down, danced or painted, can evolve its own structure, its own world. The word *create* comes from "to make grow," as in the act of cultivating plants. We grow or evolve a set of rules to incorporate the unfolding of our imagination. We create new rules of progression, fresh channels in which the play can flow.

Shaping the Whole

In free improvisation we play the sounds and silences, and as we play them they disappear forever. In producing large works—books, symphonies, plays, research projects, films—we are perforce taking the results of many inspirations and melding them together into a flowing structure that has its own integrity and endures through time. The most ephemeral thoughts and feelings are gradually shaped into hard copy that is worked over, painted over, edited, and refined before the public sees it. This is where the sculptor cuts away and polishes the stone; where the painter covers the beginnings of the image with layer upon layer of enriching re-vision.

The muse presents raw bursts of inspiration, flashes, and improvisatory moments in which the art just flows out. But she also presents the technical, organizational job of taking what we have generated, then filing and fitting and playing with the pieces until they line up. We arrange them, cook them, render them down, digest them. We add, subtract, reframe, shift, break apart, melt together. The play of revision and editing transforms the raw into the cooked. This is a whole art unto itself, of vision and revision, playing again with the half-baked products of our prior play.

It is essential to perform that secretarial labor in a way that is not mechanical. Editing must come from the same inspired joy and abandon as free improvisation. Stravinsky tells us, "The idea of work to be done is for me so closely bound up with the idea of the arranging of materials and of the pleasure that the actual doing of the work affords us that, should the impossible happen and my work suddenly be given to me in a perfectly completed form, I should be embarrassed and nonplussed by it, as by a hoax."[33]

There is a stereotyped belief that the muse in us acts from inspiration, while the editor in us acts from reason and judgment. But if we leave our imp or improviser out of the process, re-vision becomes impossible. If I see the paragraph I wrote last month as mere words on a page, they become dead and so do I. But if I look at them sideways, do a little *disappearing,* they begin to slither and grow tentacles like primitive living things; the tentacles begin to link up with each other, to hook and unhook, until a pattern appears and clarifies itself.

The evolving organism takes on a momentum and identity of its own. We conduct a dialogue with the living work in progress. We need not be shy about talking out loud to our work. Generally we regard talking to oneself out loud as a sign of lunacy, and answering oneself back a sign of even worse lunacy; but in the case of creative bafflement this is a very valuable technique. Just get away from other people for a while so you can do it undisturbed. At crucial times this inner dialogue becomes the core of the creative process.

Some elements of artistic editing: (1) deep feeling for the intentions beneath the surface; (2) sensual love of the language; (3) sense of elegance; and (4) ruthlessness. The first three can perhaps be summarized under the category of good taste, which involves sensation, sense of balance, and knowledge of the medium, leavened with an appropriate sense of outrageousness. Ruthlessness is necessary in order to keep the artwork clear and simple—but note that there is a gigantic difference between simplicity and insipidity! The simple formulation of our vision may be far from easy; it may be challenging and disturbing and demand a great deal of work.

In the tricky business of fitting the pieces together, we work from a double point of view, moving deductively from our original inspiration of the whole and inductively from our particular inspirations of detail. Sometimes what's needed is to crudely smash through the confusions and obstacles; sometimes the most delicate, patient, intermittent massaging of the problem. Sometimes it is we ourselves who need to be hit over the head or gently massaged. Sometimes the pieces we love most are the ones that end up on the cutting room floor. They may be some of the first-born images upon which the whole work was built. But when a building is completed, the scaffolding must come down.

By manipulating and massaging form, we perform a sympathetic magic on the spiritual insides of our work; we evolve shapes and structures and live by them. We may write poetry in a traditional form, like a sonnet or haiku; or we may invent our own form, perhaps to use only once for a single poem, perhaps to develop through our lifetime as a personal style. We may go for free verse, which implies a lack of form, but it too is a definite game that the poet consciously enters into, carrying its own responsibilities. "To live outside the law," sang Bob Dylan, "you must be honest."[34]

Once the first raw draft of a poem emerges, the poet enters into a jigsaw game, playing with the line breaks, with the placement of stressed and unstressed syllables. There come many lines and phrases that seem quite lovely, quite right—but they don't fit with the rhythm and shape of what's already there. The editing process, of threshing out, reshaping, breaking, lengthening the phrases until they come out whole, may sound like imposing a tyranny of form—

wouldn't it be better to be free? But in fact the opposite is true. As the form refines the feeling, the poem just gets better and better, truer to the original, unnameable feeling at its source. This is one of the most delightful aspects of art making. There comes a moment when the whole thing slides into shape—you can almost hear the click—when the feeling and the form come into a state of harmony. The impact of this seemingly abstract process is immediate and physiological. For me, tears flow, I get a gigantic surge of energy, and if I leave my studio and go outdoors I find that I am actually floating.

Why this surge of emotion? I believe that the tears are tears of *recognition;* by wrestling with a new feeling and a new form until they fit one another, I find that I have uncovered a very old feeling, something that has been with me forever but that has never before surfaced. Fitting the feeling together with the form, re-saying and reworking the poem many times, elicits aspects of the feeling that I would never have thought of if I had expressed it in just any form at all. When it all slides into place, at those moments when the tears come, what I sense is not merely the satisfaction of accomplishment but rather a direct realization that the world is one and I've connected with the world. A shock of recognition: I've been carrying around for my whole life a feeling, a form I always knew was there—recognizing something very old in myself.

Obstacles and Openings

Childhood's End

*The creative artist and poet and saint must fight the
actual (as opposed to ideal) gods of our society—
the god of conformism as well as the gods of apathy,
material success, and exploitative power. These are
the "idols" of our society that are worshiped by
multitudes of people.*

ROLLO MAY

At the age of four, a child I knew drew extraordinarily vibrant, imaginative trees. Crayon, chalk, colored
pens, and silly putty were all useful. These trees were remarkable in how clearly they showed the bulbous lobes and
branchy veins of individual leaves in a kind of cubist, all-the-way-around view that would have delighted Picasso. Meticulous observation of real trees, and a certain daring that is
characteristic of four-year-olds, combined to produce these
striking artworks.

By the age of six, this child had gone through a year of
first grade and had begun drawing lollipop trees just like
the other kids. Lollipop trees consist of a single blob of
green, representing the general mass of leaves with details
obliterated, stuck up on top of a brown stick, representing
the tree trunk. Not the sort of place real frogs would live.

Another child, age eight, complained of the day her
third-grade teacher pretended that negative numbers don't
exist. While the class was doing subtraction tables, a boy
asked, "What's 3 take-away 5?" and the teacher insisted that
there is no such thing. The girl objected, "But everyone
knows it's minus 2!" The schoolteacher said, "This is the

third grade and you're not supposed to know about those things!"

I later asked this girl, "What does a minus number mean to you?" She said without hesitating, "It's like looking at your reflection in a pool of water. It goes as far down as you go up." This is original mind in action, the purest form of Zen.

This clear, deep voice is latent in us from earliest childhood, but it is latent only. The adventures, difficulties, and even suffering inherent in growing up can serve to develop or educe our original voice, but more often they bury it. It may be developed or undeveloped, excited or inhibited, by the way we are raised and trained and treated in life.[35] Because most of our institutions are built on the Lockean fantasy that the newborn person is a *tabula rasa* on which knowledge is built up like a pyramid, we tend to erase our children's innate from-the-top-down knowledge and try to fill them

instead with simplistic bottoms-up knowledge. "As up I grew," wrote e. e. cummings, "Down I forgot."[36]

Schools can nurture creativity in children, but they can also destroy it, and all too often do. Ideally, schools exist to preserve and regenerate learning and the arts, to give children the tools with which they may create the future. At worst, they produce uniform, media-minded grown-ups to feed the marketplace with workers, with managers, and with consumers.

The child we were and are learns by exploring and experimenting, insistently snooping into every little corner that is open to us—and into the forbidden corners too! But sooner or later our wings get clipped. The real world created by grown-ups comes to bear down upon growing children, molding them into progressively more predictable members of society. This devolutionary process is reinforced throughout the life cycle, from kindergarten through university, in social and political life, and most especially in the world of work. Our newest and most powerful educational institutions, television and pop music, are even more thorough than school in inculcating mass-produced conformity. People are grown as a kind of food to be gobbled up by the system. Slowly our eyes begin to narrow. Thus the simplicity, intelligence, and power of mind at play become homogenized into complexity, conformity, and weakness.

We need to recognize that every bit of our culture is school; we are presented moment to moment with affirmations of some realities and denials of others. Education, business, media, politics, and above all the family, the very institutions that might be the instruments for expanding human expressiveness, collude to induce conformism, to keep things going on a humdrum level. But so do our everyday habits of doing or seeing. Reality as we know it becomes conditioned by the tacit assumptions we come to take for granted after innumerable subtle learning experiences in daily life. That is why creative perceptions seem extraordinary or special to us, when in fact creativity is usually a matter of seeing through those tacit assumptions to what is right in front of our noses. A story is told of a French railroad passenger who, upon learning that his neighbor on the next seat was Picasso, began to grouse and grumble about modern art, saying that it is not a faithful representation of reality. Picasso demanded to know what was a faithful representation of reality. The man produced a wallet-sized photo and said, "There! That's a real picture—that's what my wife really looks like." Picasso looked at it carefully from several angles, turning it up and down and sideways, and said, "She's awfully small. And flat."

We often make the mistake of confusing education with training, when in fact these are very different activities. Training is for the purpose of passing on specific information necessary to perform a specialized activity. Education is the building of the person. To *educe* means to draw out or evoke that which is latent; education then means drawing out the person's latent capacities for understanding and living, not stuffing a (passive) person full of preconceived knowledge. Education must tap into the close relationship between play and exploration; there must be permission to explore and express. There must be validation of the exploratory spirit, which by definition takes us out of the tried, the tested, and the homogeneous.

The conformity that is taught by the big school that surrounds us resembles what biologists call monoculture: If you walk in a wild field you see dozens of different species of grasses, mosses, and other turf in each square yard, as well as a rich supply of tiny animals. This is nature's insurance that changes in climate and environment will be matched by requisite variety in the plant life. But if you walk in a domesticated field you will see only one or a few species. Domesticated animals and plants are genetically uniform because they are bred for a purpose. Diversity and flexibility are bred out in exchange for maximizing certain variables that suit our purpose. But if conditions change, the species is locked into a narrow range of variety. Monoculture leads invariably to a loss of options, which leads to instability.

Monoculture is anathema to learning. The exploratory spirit thrives on variety and free play—but many of our institutions manage to kill it by putting it into small boxes. They tend to divide learning into specializations and departments. A certain amount of specialization is necessary to handle any large task, or any large body of knowledge. But the barriers we set up between specialties tend to become overdeveloped. The professions acquire an inertial mass that deadens everything they touch. We confront a proliferation of disciplines and -ologies, most of which function primarily to protect their own professional turf. We fragment learning at the expense of the richness and flexibility that should be inherent in a living body of knowledge.

One of the many catch-22's in the business of creativity is that you can't express inspiration without skill, but if you are too wrapped up in the professionalism of skill you obviate the surrender to accident that is essential to inspiration. You begin to emphasize product at the expense of process. It is possible for an artist to have stupendous technical prowess, to be able to amaze and delight audiences with dazzling virtuosity, and yet there is—something lacking. We all at one time or another have had the experience of hearing a fantastically impressive performance of a concerto, in which this mysterious something is not there. The superficial brilliance pulls an automatic reaction ("Wow!") from us—it's like meeting a beautiful person of the opposite sex who turns out to have no brain, or no heart. One instinctively says this "Wow!" in some form or other, even if on second look there's not much there.

On the other hand, most of us have also had the experience of hearing an unsophisticated performance that may be full of wrong notes, or a piece of child-song, or a performance by a street musician in which we are moved to tears, immobilized with a palpable feeling of awe. There is something godlike about these rare and special performances, something that cannot be intended. "Like a god" means that the listener feels he is in the presence of raw creative power, the primal force that made us. That is what a god does: create. He takes us back to origins, as did Einstein in returning to such basic and childish matters as learning about space and time and looking at them freshly:

The normal adult never troubles his head about space-time problems. Everything there is to be thought about, in his opinion, has already been done in early childhood. I, on the contrary, developed so slowly that I only began to wonder about space and time when I was already grown up.[37]

The professionalism of technique and the flash of dexterity are more comfortable to be around than raw creative power; hence our society generally rewards virtuoso performers more highly than it rewards original creators. It is relatively easy to judge and evaluate technical brilliance. Spiritual and emotional content are not so easy to evaluate. They are intuited directly, subtly, and often become apparent to the world at large only after a considerable passage of time.

The worst piece Beethoven ever wrote, the boring and pompous *Battle Symphony,* was the most popular in his own lifetime. Bach's *Brandenburg Concertos,* now among the most beloved music of all time, were sent off to the Margrave of Brandenburg as supporting material for a job application. Bach did not get the job. Bizet lived for only a year after the premiere of *Carmen.* During that time the opera was a failure, roundly condemned for its lack of accessible melody.

There are certainly exceptions to these ironies as well. Some artists have the good fortune of presenting revolutionary, original work, yet being perfectly in tune with their times.

It is not always true that the books, the music, the movies, the TV shows that sell well are trashy or mindless, but it is true often enough. Artists who want and need to sell their work may thus be afflicted by no less than two judging spectres. One spectre whispers menacingly in the right ear, "Is this good enough?" The other whispers menacingly in the left ear, "Is this commercial enough?" This tension reflects the values of a society that considers the product more important than the process. What's wanted is a sure thing, the assurance that we are getting a product whose value has been ratified by the authorities. None of this can be specified a priori if we are dealing with raw creativity.

We block creativity by labeling it as unusual, extraordinary, segregating it into special realms like art and science. We segregate it further from ordinary life by establishing systems of star performers. The value of one's work is not dependent on its quality but on one's name. In 1988, van Gogh, who could not sell a painting in his lifetime, sold, as a dead man, two paintings for fifty million dollars apiece. If an artist becomes a star—or even better, a dead star—he or she becomes an identifiable product that can be packaged. When an artist changes and develops over the years, as is natural to any creative person, such change is met by howls of protest from the marketers. Sometimes an artist (or teacher, scientist, or spiritual guru) starts with something extraordinary, becomes a star, and then their gift is either frozen or perverted.

The growing and risky edge of creative work is devalued, treated as a frill or extracurricular activity decorating the routine of ordinary life. There are few mechanisms available for the artist to construct a self-sustaining way of living and working. "One gathers," says Virginia Woolf,

> from the enormous modern literature of confession and self-analysis that to write a work of genius is almost always a feat of prodigious difficulty. Everything is against the likelihood that it will come from the writer's mind whole and entire. Generally material circumstances are against it. Dogs will bark; people will interrupt; money must be made; health will break down. Further, accentuating all these difficulties and making them harder to bear is the world's notorious indifference. It does not ask people to write poems and novels and histories; it does not need them. It does not care whether

Flaubert finds the right word or whether Carlyle scrupulously
verifies this or that fact. Naturally, it will not pay for what it
does not want. And so the writer, Keats, Flaubert, Carlyle,
suffers, especially in the creative years of youth, every form
of distraction and discouragement. A curse, a cry of agony,
rises from those books of analysis and confession. "Mighty
poets in their misery dead"—that is the burden of their song.
If anything comes through in spite of all this, it is a miracle,
and probably no book is born entire and uncrippled as it was
conceived.[38]

It sometimes seems as though there were a vast unconscious collusion of our institutions to constrain the normal
mode in which we conduct our lives into a kind of blocked
and rigid mold. We suppress, deny, rationalize, forget the
muse's messages, because we are told that the voice of inner
knowing is not real. When we fear the power of the life force
we become stuck in the dull round of conventional responses. "Something lacking!" The frozen state of apathy,
conformism, and confusion is normative, but must not be
taken as normal. Everyone gets cavities and colds, but that
does not make them normal or desirable. Creative living, or
the life of a creator, seems like a leap into the unknown only
because "normal life" is rigid and traumatized.

It is easy to look around us and see innumerable factors
that undermine the creative life. But I think every culture
contains its own defenses against creativity. It is sometimes
tempting to idealize or romanticize some other time and
place where the creative life seems to have been more integrated into the fabric of life as a whole. I've met artists who
wished they could have lived in the Renaissance; but in the
Renaissance artists viewed themselves as the degenerate descendants of ancient Greece; and the Greeks saw themselves
as degenerate descendants of a long-gone Golden Age
(probably Cretan); and so on.

Aaron Copland drops an interesting remark while telling us what it felt like to be a composer in America in the early part of this century. Art, music, and literature were treated, then as now, as frills. Concert music was listened to by only a tiny part of society, and that part wanted to hear only European masters, not American music or new music; and classical-music audiences then as now believed that the only good composer was a dead composer. This was even more true in the 1920s, when Copland was developing his art, than today. But instead of complaining, he tells us, "The fun of the fight against the musical Philistines, the sorties and strategies, the converts won, and the hot arguments with dull-witted critics partly explain the particular excitements of that period."[39] That attitude takes all the crassness and stupidity of the world and makes it the occasion for a game. This is pearl making at its best. Copland's remark indicates that whatever he may find in the world, if a creative person has a sense of humor, a sense of style, and a certain amount of stubbornness, he finds a way to do what he needs to in spite of the obstacles. (Independent wealth helps too.)

But we have not yet gotten down to the marrow of the matter. We have been talking as though there were something called "society" that defends itself against creativity by all the means we've mentioned above: education, specialization, fear of the new, fear of raw creative power. There is no such thing as society, there is no such thing as institutions, schools, the media, and the rest of it. There are only people doing their imperfect best at doing their imperfect jobs. The marrow of the matter is that however we might restructure society, however many resources an enlightened regime might bestow on the fostering of creativity and the arts and sciences and freewheeling education dedicated to the deep exploration of mind, spirit, and heart, we would still be in the same soup. There is something called growing up, which happens to us no matter what our circumstances. We all have

learned what it feels like to be betrayed for the first time, the second time, the third time, when our innocence gets stripped away, and we jump from innocence to experience. There is a point, or rather a long series of points, at which our innocence and free play of imagination and desire collides with reality, with the limits of is and is not, with the limits of what can and cannot be.

Everything we have said so far should not be construed merely as an indictment of the big bad schools, or the media or other societal factors. We could redesign many aspects of society in a more wholesome way—and we ought to—but even then art would not be easy. The fact is that we cannot avoid childhood's end; the free play of imagination creates illusions, and illusions bump into reality and get disillusioned. Getting disillusioned, presumably, is a fine thing, the essence of learning; but it hurts. If you think that you could have avoided the disenchantment of childhood's end by having had some advantage—a more enlightened education, more money or other material benefits, a great teacher—talk to someone who has had those advantages, and you will find that they bump into just as much disillusionment because the fundamental blockages are not external but part of us, part of life. In any case, the child's delightful pictures of trees mentioned at the beginning of this chapter would probably not be art if they came from the hands of an adult. The difference between the child's drawings and the childlike drawing of a Picasso resides not only in Picasso's impeccable mastery of craft, but in the fact that Picasso had actually grown up, undergone hard experience, and transcended it.

Vicious Circles

Sometimes, when I find I haven't written a single sentence after scribbling whole pages, I collapse on my couch and lie there dazed, bogged in a swamp of despair, hating myself and blaming myself for this demented pride that makes me pout after a chimera. A quarter of an hour later, everything has changed; my heart is pounding with joy.

GUSTAVE FLAUBERT

The creative processes of free play and concentrated practice can be derailed. They can go spinning off into addiction or procrastination, into obsession or obstruction, leaving us, outside our own natural flow of activity, in states of confusion and self-doubt. Addiction is excessive, compulsive attachment; procrastination is excessive, compulsive avoidance.

Addiction is any dependency that self-perpetuates or self-catalyzes at an ever-accelerating rate. It accounts for much of the suffering we inflict on ourselves and each other. There are addictions to drugs, to lifestyles, to the affection of another person, to knowledge, to having more and more weapons, or to a higher and higher gross national product. There are addictions to outmoded dogmas, for which people are still massacring each other the world over. There are addictions to success and to failure. Frustrating events in our lives can also touch off addictions to obsessive thoughts, which we cannot leave alone and on which we compulsively gnaw.

An artist can be addicted to an idea, stuck in a particular

self-concept, a particular view of how the work must go, or what the audience may want.

Some habits may appear in both addictive and nonaddictive (normal) forms. Some habits may seem addictive, such as physical exercise or practicing a musical instrument, or doing some other labor of love, yet we may consider them to be positive and beneficial. There is a fine line between the pathological and the creative, between addiction and practice. What actually is the vital difference between "I'll just have one more drink" and "I'll just try that Bach fugue one more time"?

Addiction consumes energy and leads to slavery. Practice generates energy and leads to freedom. In practice, or in creative reading or listening, we obsess in order to find out more and more, as in the Twenty Questions game. In addiction, we obsess in order to avoid finding out something, or in order to avoid facing something unpleasant. In practice the act becomes more and more expansive; we are unwinding a thread outward and building more and more implications and connections. In addiction we are folding inward, into more sameness, more dullness.

Habits are addictive if that mysterious acceleration factor is present, when enough is never enough, and what was enough yesterday is not enough today. Habits are addictive if the reward and the work are inverted. Samuel Butler joked that if the alcoholic's hangover preceded the intoxication, there would be mystical schools teaching it as a discipline for self-realization. So practice is the reciprocal of addiction. Practice is an ever-fresh, challenging flow of work and play in which we continually test and demolish our own delusions; therefore it is sometimes painful.

Addiction is what computer programmers call a "do-loop." Self-regulating beings, whether animals, people, or ecosystems, spend much of their time performing repetitive routines. Built into the structure of such routines are end-conditions or exits. We keep performing the routine until the end-condition indicates that the job is done. Pouring tea, we monitor for the condition "Is the cup full?" That condition turns off the act of pouring. Eating, we continue until certain autonomic signs (stomach bulk, blood sugar, and so on) feed back the message that we are full. Normally, we then stop. But it is possible for the end-condition to be omitted, misplaced, or for the signals to be switched, so that the routine is carried out indefinitely, compulsively, until all sorts of disorders, explosions, or breakdowns bring the whole system to a halt.

If addiction is a form of do-loop, from which there is no exit, procrastination is a don't-loop, which consists of nothing but exit. In a circle of addictive feedback, we believe "The more the merrier." Under stress, such a belief can accelerate into a do-loop, which drives us into an explosive runaway, such as an eating or drinking binge, a population explosion, an arms race. In procrastination we believe "The less the safer." This, under stress, drives us into a don't-loop, a cycle of compression or blockage, like a muscle spasm, writer's block, sexual impotence, depression, anomie, or catatonia. In this kind of vicious circle the exit condition fires off continuously, never allowing us to maintain the activity. This state gives rise to procrastination, and all the other inverse addictions, the addictions to not-doing, the blocks, the allergies.

Procrastination is the mirror image of addiction; both are disorders of self-regulation. We are stuck in these cycles unless and until we can find the crossed signal and switch it back again.

As living beings, we are naturally self-regulating and self-balancing, but in addition we have consciousness, with its attendant functions of pride, selective awareness, linear thinking, and ego maintenance. The profound difference between these two tendencies involves us in certain contradictions and difficulties. Consider what happens when you steer a car. Your hands-and-brain (the pilot) and your eyes-and-brain (the navigator) are engaged in a continuous dialogue that goes something like this: "We're 2° off course to the left." "Turning right." "We're 1.3° off to the right." "Turning left." "We're 1.5° off to the left." "Turning right." The car is slightly off course at any particular moment, but you usually manage to drive it straight down the roadway. The same goes for the thermostat at home, which doesn't keep the room at the desired temperature, but rather performs a continuous vibrato around the desired temperature. Likewise for the cardiovascular thermostat that regulates body temperature, and all the other homeostatic balancing acts that keep our levels of blood sugar, water, sleep, and so on in a state of dynamic health. It is a continuous dance of self-correcting play through the power of mistakes.

In a healthy feedback system, trial and error have an easy, flowing relationship, and we correct ourselves without a thought. Most of the body's feedback loops are unconscious, for the very good reason that continuous judgments of value must take effect without delay, interference, or clenching caused by ego attachment. Even a complex and highly voluntary activity like driving a car is usually performed unconsciously, without thinking about it; yet our attention is monitoring thousands of acts and conditions per minute. But if steering a car were like some of our more conscious processes, the inner dialogue between hand and eye might go very differently: "We're 2° off course to the left." "OK, I'll fix it." "We're 1.3° off to the right." "Yes, I heard you!" "We're 1.5° off to the left." "Damn you, stop telling me what to do!"

The extra piece that consciousness puts in is the attachment of ego to one side or the other. The ego wants to be right, but in the dynamics of life and art we are never right, we are always changing and cycling. This attachment to one

pole of a dynamic cycle sets us up for all the afflictive emotions: anger, pride, envy. If one pole or the other exerts an
inordinate pull on us, we can't steer because we have no
center. This is especially true if the attachment is based in
unconscious drives or unresolved issues in our personal life.
This is why sex in advertising is so effective—it feeds upon
attachments and desires that are part of our innate makeup.

On the other hand, if one pole holds something we fear,
we will run circles around ourselves to avoid it. This pro-
longs the fear endlessly. If I am obsessed by a thought or a
pain, the only way out is to go right into the source of the
pain and find out what piece of information is dying to express itself.

Another variant of the steering story occurs when we
become sticky, and the ego tracks or attaches to the back-and-
forth movements. Then we are blown back and forth in
waves of indecision. "We're 2° too left." "I want left!"
"We're 1.3° right." "I want right!" This leads to another
manifestation of the don't-loop—nervous fidgeting and all
activities that expend energy at cross-purposes to our chosen
direction.

Some people find it easier to play a violin concerto or
to make or lose a million dollars than to sit still for thirty
minutes.

"Fidget" comes from an Old Norse word that means
"to desire eagerly." Fidgeting and boredom are the symptoms of fear of emptiness, which we try to fill up with whatever we can lay our hands on. We are taught to be bored,
to seek easy entertainment, to ardently desire the ephemeral.
There are multibillion-dollar industries—television, alcohol,
tobacco, drugs—based on feeding this fear of emptiness.
They provide opportunities for our eyes and brains to fidget
and forget. Shorter and shorter attention spans are inculcated
in us by the rhythms of society, which become increasingly

nervous and jittery, which shorten our attention spans further—another vicious circle.

Just as free play on the violin is impeded by involuntary contractions of the voluntary muscles, spasms lasting mere tenths of a second, free play in daily life is impeded by short-term compulsive activities, little movements that fritter away energy, physical symptoms of nervousness and indecision, like crossing and uncrossing of legs, changes of posture, chewing of lips. Or these movements may take place over minutes in the form of changing your *mind,* U-turns in the car, driving in circles. Or you may undertake a really long-term activity, like a job or a marriage that does not accord with your inner nature, as a form of fidgeting.

Underneath procrastination and fidgeting lies self-doubt. Self-doubt appends a little superscripted "but on the other hand, maybe not" to every impulse we have. We then find ourselves gnawing on each decision, changing course, retracing our steps again and again.

Consciousness may interfere with a naturally self-guiding system not only through pride but through desperation as well. It can be profoundly depressing to seem to be off-course all the time. Self-doubt undermines the normally automatic self-balancing that makes life possible. Blake said, "If the sun and moon should doubt, they'd immediately go out!"[40] Hence another variant of the pilot-and-navigator metaphor: "We're 2° off course to the left." "Oh, I'm sorry!" "We're 1.3° off to the right." "Oh, I'm a failure!" "We're 1.5° off to the left." "Oh God, I'm going to kill myself!" This scenario may seem humorous, but we can read in it the real sufferings and sometimes the real suicides of many artists.

To summarize the steerage metaphor, we can say that the inevitable back-and-forth vibrato of feedback can be experienced in different states of mind: self-trimming practice; addiction (compulsively sticking to one side of the scale) or procrastination (compulsively avoiding one side of the scale); wandering desires (avidly attaching to each passing state, or fidgeting); anger (resenting the changes); spiritual or real suicide (self-doubt).

The fundamental thing about vicious circles, by definition, is that there is no logical way out. No matter which way we turn, we are stuck in the loop of doing or not doing, of being or seeing in a certain way, until our options narrow and finally disappear. There is no logical way out; but fortunately there *are* a number of nonlogical ways out. Before we look at these we need to look at what underlies the vicious circles—fear.

The Judging Spectre

Each man is in his spectre's power
Until the arrival of that hour
When his Humanity awake
And cast his spectre into the lake.
WILLIAM BLAKE

When the creative processes grind to a halt, we have that unbearable feeling of being totally clogged, we suffer the antithesis of the shiny, alert mentality described above as "disappearing." Instead of experiencing relaxed, energetic concentration, we jump avidly toward any distraction, no matter how trivial or ridiculous; we become easily tired; when we look back at our work nothing seems good enough; our eyelids glaze over; our brain cells chug to a standstill.

The creative person can be seen as embodying or acting as two inner characters, a muse and an editor. These are the pilot and navigator of the last chapter, seen from a different angle. The muse proposes, the editor disposes. The editor criticizes, shapes, and organizes the raw material that the free play of the muse has generated. If, however, the editor precedes rather than follows the muse, we have trouble. The artist judges his work before there is yet anything to judge, and this produces a blockage or paralysis. The muse gets edited right out of existence.

If he gets out of control, the inner critic can be experienced as a harsh and punishing father figure. This is the inhibiting spectre who haunts the lives of many artists, an invisible, critical, bullying force that seems to stand in our way.

As our artwork flows out from its mysterious source, it becomes objective, something that can be heard, evaluated, explored, experimented upon. In art we are continually judging our work, continually tracking the patterns we create and letting our judgments feed back into the ongoing development. The music is self-monitoring, self-regulating, self-judging. That's how we produce art rather than chaos; that's how evolution produces an organism rather than a heap of randomized carbon, nitrogen, oxygen, hydrogen, sulfur, sodium, and other atoms.

But there are two kinds of judgment: *con*structive and *ob*structive. Constructive judgment moves right along with the time of creation as a continuous feedback, a kind of parallel track of consciousness that facilitates the action. Obstructive judgment runs, as it were, perpendicular to the line of action, interposing itself before creation (writer's block) or after creation (rejection or indifference). The trick for the creative person is to be able to tell the difference between the two kinds of judgment and cultivate constructive judgment.

This means telling the difference between two kinds of time. The feedback between constructive judgment and the ongoing creative work goes back and forth at more than lightning speed: it goes on in no-time (eternity). The partners, muse and editor, are always in synchrony, like a pair of dancers who have known each other for a long time.

When judgment is obstructive, occurring perpendicular to the flow of our work rather than parallel with it, our personal time is chopped into segments, and each segment is a possible stopping point, an opportunity for confusion and self-doubt to sneak in. To either like or dislike our work for more than a moment can be dangerous. The judging voice asks, "Is this good enough?" But even if we create something really stupendous, sooner or later we have to perform again, and that inner judging voice is back again, saying, "It had better be better than the last time." Thus one's very talent can be a factor in blocking creativity. Either success or failure can turn that voice on.

The easiest way to do art is to dispense with success and failure altogether and just get on with it.

Thus Seng-Tsan writes in the eighth century, "The Way [the Great Tao] is not difficult, just avoid picking and choosing."[41] But this is easier to say than to practice. We are assaulted by the pushes and pulls of desire, aversion, and vascillation, and all the afflictive emotions that accompany them. The afflictive emotions include envy, anger, greed, and self-importance, but their root—like the root of addiction, procrastination, and other forms of blockage—is fear.

Buddhists speak of the Five Fears that stand between ourselves and our freedom: fear of loss of life; fear of loss of livelihood; fear of loss of reputation; fear of unusual states of mind; and fear of speaking before an assembly. Fear of speaking before an assembly sounds a little silly next to the others, but for the purposes of *Free Play* it is the central one; let us extend it as "fear of speaking up," "stage fright," "writer's block," and our other old friends. The fear is profoundly related to fear of foolishness, which has two parts: fear of being thought a fool (loss of reputation) and fear of actually being a fool (fear of unusual states of mind).

Let's add fear of ghosts. One of the blocking bugaboos is being overwhelmed by teachers, authorities, parents, or the great masters. Deviation from the true self often arises from comparison with or envy of the idealized other (parent, lover, teacher, past master, hero). Geniuses or stars are set up as unattainable goals we cannot possibly match. These personalities are so much more spectacular than you that you might as well keep your mouth shut to begin with. We may fear the ghosts of our parental or teacher figures, but also the

ghosts of great creators of the past. Brahms feared that he could not measure up to the ghost of Beethoven; so may a contemporary symphonic composer fear the ghost of Brahms. Brahms couldn't finish his first symphony for twenty-two years because he had a monkey on his back called Beethoven. He wrote to his friend Herman Levi in 1874, "You don't know what it feels like to be dogged by that giant!"

It's great to sit on the shoulders of giants, but don't let the giants sit on *your* shoulders! There's no room for their legs to dangle.

So we meet perfectionism and its ugly twin, procrastination. We need to do everything, have everything, be everything. Perfectionism arrests us perhaps more effectively than any other block. It brings us face to face with our judging spectre, and since we can't possibly measure up, we sit in a funk of procrastination. We generate an unproductive anti-dote to these feelings of envy: fantasies of omnipotence or fabulous success, or else their inverse, victim or bad-luck fantasies.

Another bugaboo is fear of being perceived as arrogant or out of the ordinary. We can be taught by our peers in school that if we excel intellectually, or even more so artistically, we are liable to be isolated from society. Fear of success can be as potent as fear of failure. Parents may foster this fear. They may encourage a child to excel, but only along accepted lines. The child may be haunted by fear that if he expresses himself in his own way he is not going to be loved or accepted for who he is. All too often this is not only a fear but a reality.

There may also be multiple ghosts of ourselves hanging around, all the people we might have been if the past had taken a different turn; we should have, could have, would have done *x*. We all indulge in this sort of self-torture from time to time. What can save us is our knowledge that true creativity arises from *bricolage,* from working with whatever odd assortment of funny-shaped materials we have at hand, including our odd assortment of funny-shaped selves.

No matter how advanced we may become, we fear that people will find us out as fakes. There were so many times, when I was involved in the teaching profession, that I would have a room full of students sitting round a table, each one feeling that he or she was the only one who didn't get it, and therefore ashamed to speak up. Fear of foolishness and fear of mistakes tap into that very primal feeling we all learned as children: shame. Then the moment would come when someone did speak up, after which a second person felt safe and also spoke up, with a "I thought I was the only one who felt that way"; then everyone would reveal similar feelings (including myself!). Only when we were finally and thoroughly comfortable with the fact that we were all equal in being three-thumbed ignoramuses could the shared work of learning begin in earnest.

The judging spectre often appears in the guise of some external impediment, involving money, fashion, political factors, or the world's seeming indifference to creative expression. Even our loved ones can take on this role. We feel like victims of circumstances beyond our control, a malevolent fate, a rival, or some petty tyrant who has entered our lives. At such moments the power of play seems to be stopped dead in its tracks. Childhood's end is the encounter with "hard reality"—this is the source of our myths about the Fall from primeval Paradise. The supports of hard reality are fear of judgment, fear of failure, and frustration; these are society's defenses against creativity.

We see now that to a certain extent we can identify the mysterious spectre as the self-clinging habits of being that we reify as the ego. The spectre is what psychoanalysts call an introject—or rather it is the sum total of all the introjects. It is our automatic internalization of the parental and other judging voices that throw doubt on whether we are good enough, smart enough, the right size or shape; and also of the wishful voices that indicate who we should be and what we should like to have. Both hope and fear are functions of the judging spectre. As we grow, certain injunctions of these voices stick to us, and thus the "me" or little self is built up, layer by layer. The spectre is always looking out for number one. He worries about survival, competition, and pride. The Sufis call him the *Nafs* within each of us; many of their practices are aimed at subduing or taming him. Blake called the judging spectre Urizen—"your reason," the jealous rational power untamed by love, imagination, and humor. Urizen's principal (and only) weapon is fear. No matter what the external circumstances of our life, this fear is internally fed, imposed by one part of ourselves onto another.

The judging spectre gives these fears a familiar face and personifies them —perhaps as the parent, the teacher, the boss, the political tyrant. It is exceedingly easy for us to externalize him, to reify him, to turn him into the Other or the Enemy, to look for him outside ourselves in all the

persons or factors that may be putting us down, getting in our way. We can spend a lifetime searching him out and blaming everyone and everything around us for the frustrations of our blocked creative voice. Under such circumstances, it can become an unbearable burden to say anything at all. We become tied up in knots of paradox looking for the entity that is blocking us up. It is like looking for fire with a lighted match.

Surrender

The intuition discovered, the unconscious made conscious, is always a surprise. Time after time my best music comes when I feel that the material is played out; I am at the end of my resources, and the piece had better end before I make a fool of myself. So I grope toward a closing phrase, and finish—but somehow, despite my intent, the bow refuses to stop! The cadence or whatever ending I contrive modulates into something else, and out of nowhere comes a totally new melody. I feel in my blood, my bones, my muscles, my brain, a wholly new and unexpected surge of energy. This is the second wind. Time doubles and triples over on itself; *I* disappear and the music really starts to cook. My feeling is invariably one of wonderment: "How in hell did *that* happen? I didn't know I had *that* in me!" Suddenly we, the players and the listeners, find ourselves elsewhere; the music has *moved* us.

Slowly, as I accumulated more and more of these experiences, I came to feel comfortable relinquishing a certain degree of control. I began to play as if the bow itself were making the music, and my job was simply to stay out of its way. I allowed the violin its own life and gratefully receded into the background. I no longer sought skill, flexibility, strength, endurance, muscle tone, and quick responsiveness as means of imposing my will on the instrument, but rather of keeping open an unrestricted pathway for the creative impulse to play its music straight from the preconscious depths beneath and beyond me. I came to know that blocks are the price of avoiding surrender, and that surrender is not defeat but rather the key to opening out into a world of delight and nonstop creation.

One of the great traps at times of blockage is that we may accuse ourselves of a deficit of concentration and focus, a deficit of discipline. We then take a paternal or militaristic attitude toward ourselves. We will *force* ourselves to work, we will go on a schedule, we will take vows. The most dangerous trap is to get into a contest of strength between "will power" and "won't power." Discipline is crucial, but we do not attain it by stiffening up. We attain it by sitting still and penetrating the emptiness within, making of that emptiness a friend rather than an adversary or bogeyman.

When you are stuck, meditate, free associate, do automatic writing, talk to yourself and answer yourself. Play *with* the blocks. Stay in the *temenos* of the workplace. Relax, surrender to the bafflement; don't leave the *temenos,* and the solution will come. Persevere gently. Use *intelleto,* the visionary faculty. Stay close to the zero mark; indulge neither in great highs nor in great lows.

The depths are obscured in us when we try to force feelings; we clarify them by giving them adequate time and space and letting them come. What we experienced yesterday as the pride of creativity or the self-deprecating feeling of incapacity we see today as the signal to surrender.

Like the rules of the universe, the whole matter of personal creativity is baffling and paradoxical. To *try* to control yourself, to *try* to create, to *try* to break free of the knots you yourself have tied is to set yourself up at a distance from that which you already are. It is like looking around this way and that for your own head. It's like what happens to Zen practitioners in the thick of working on a koan, feeling as if they are trying to swallow a molten ball of red-hot iron that they cannot gulp down and cannot spit out.

I reach a point at which the complexities, contradictions, paradoxes, and impossibilities pile up so high that I become overwhelmed. I have gone through it again and again, have tried every avenue, and I meet frustration at every point. Finally the only way left is to stand up and burst out of the armor. I am stuck, I have to do something, I am on the edge of a cliff. I may as well jump. Suddenly I don't care if I ever solve this enigma; I'm alive, to hell with it. Somehow, by jumping, by tossing out the whole mass of tangled paradoxes but retaining my aliveness, something inside me gives way. Out of this jump something new is born. Then the next day, as I am walking down the street, the simple solution comes.

Although I now know that I must give up the need to control, I cannot intentionally decide to give it up, or simulate giving it up, in order to make the music rejuvenate itself out of a stuck place. That just doesn't work. The surrender has got to be genuine, uncontrived, wholehearted: I have got to really abandon all hope and fear, with nothing to gain and nothing to lose. This paradox of control versus letting things happen naturally cannot be rationalized, it can only be resolved in actual practice. Rumi writes:

> You suspect this could be yours
> with a little contrivance.
>
> Only death to contrivance
> Will avail you.
>
> Something "good" or "bad"
> Always comes out of you,
> It is agony to be still;
> The spool turns
> When mind pulls the thread.

When the kettle boils
Fire is revealed,
When the millstone turns
The river shows its power.

Put the lid on the kettle
And be filled
With the boiling of love. [42]

We split ourselves into controller and controlled. We think that the musician learns to control the violin. We say "control yourself" to the addict or procrastinator. We attempt to control our environment. This delusion arises from the fact that we speak a language that uses nouns and verbs. Thus we are predisposed to believe that the world consists of things and forces that move the things. But like any living entity, the system of musicians-plus-instruments-plus-listeners-plus-environment is an indivisible, interactive totality; there is something false about splitting it up into parts.

A horsemanship teacher I know has her beginning adult pupils ride bareback and without reins. She says she refuses to give them the physical means of controlling the horse until they first learn to control the horse without tools and aids, with gravity, weight, and thought alone. This means becoming one with the horse—loving the horse.

Playing an instrument is a sport in which we are dancing with an object that has a life of its own, partly yielding and partly resistant. As with the horse, the yielding and resistant qualities form an infinitely structured and self-maintaining pattern, which is continuously changing, moving, playing, dying, and cycling through its own life history. Linked with this instrument, with body and mind, we scout for the effortless way. When we have this relationship with our instrument, terms like *mastery* or *control* become meaningless.

We arrive at this effortless way not by mastering the instrument but by playing with it as a living partner. If I think of the violin as an object to be controlled, if I think of the piano, the pen, the paintbrush, the computer, or my body as objects to be controlled by a subject, an *I,* then by definition they are outside of me. My limited and self-limiting *I* is, of its nature, tied up in knots. Unless I surrender my identity, the instrument's identity, and the illusion of control, I can never become one with my own process, and the blocks will remain. Without surrender and trust—nothing.

We can now return with a richer and more poignant understanding to our earlier theme—to create you have to disappear. It seems paradoxical, because when I procrastinate and block, I do so out of a feeling that I haven't got anything in me; I think that I am empty of content and am just spinning my wheels. But I am not empty, I am full of shit!

This is not just a turn of phrase; it is the nub of the whole matter. When I look closely, shifting my angle of view, all my supposed emptiness in the blocked state is revealed as a gigantic, noisy mess of delusions, outmoded thought structures, desires, aversions, and confusions, half-digested memories, unfulfilled hopes and expectations. The whole mess of spiritual waste matter has got to be jettisoned. Only unconditional surrender leads to real emptiness, and from that place of emptiness I can be prolific and free.

We create and respond from the wonderful empty place that is generated when we surrender. I say "wonderful empty place," but most of us think of emptiness as terribly scary. We fill ourselves with all sorts of stimulation, keeping busy in order to avoid that unpleasant, queasy feeling of facing our own emptiness.

When we face our emptiness and look at it from the outside, it may indeed appear frightening or alarming; but when we move in and actually become empty, we're surprised to suddenly find ourselves most powerful and effec-

tive. For only empty, without entertainment or distracting internal dialogue, can we be instantaneously responsive to the sight, the sound, the feel of the work in front of us.

We abandon any image we may have of ourselves— including any and all concepts we may hold of art, spirituality, or creativity. To think consciously that we are doing spiritual art is not that different from doing art for money or fame. Any time we perform an activity for an outcome, even if it's a very high, noble, or admirable end, we are not totally *in* that activity. That is the lesson we draw from watching a child disappear in play. To dive into the instrument, to dive into the craft of acting or playing, into the micromoment, into what it's like to move our finger over the instrument, to forget mind, forget body, forget why we are doing it and who is there, is the essence of craft and the essence of doing our work as art. To the extent that we thus empty ourselves we can be spiritual artists. Unconditional surrender comes when I fully realize—not in my brain but in my bones—that what my life or art has handed me is bigger than my hands, bigger than any conscious understanding I can have of it, bigger than any capacity that is mine alone.

A monk asked Yün-Mên, the great ninth-century Chinese Zen master, "How is it when the tree withers and its leaves fall?" How is it when you are empty-handed and naked, when you have nothing to hold onto, when everything you might have relied upon falls away? Yün-Mên said, "Whole body exposed in the golden wind."[43] Yün-Mên is telling his student that this open, vulnerable state of mind need not be one of fright and powerlessness; when one surrenders in vast emptiness one is perhaps better equipped than ever to be and act in tune with the ways of the universe.

Patience

*No matter how slow the film, Spirit always stands
still long enough for the photographer It has chosen.*
MINOR WHITE

A friend who is both a psychiatrist and a psychic told me of a woman she knew who was distraught over an unrequited love affair. This woman begged my friend, "Can't you concoct some kind of love potion?" My friend said, "Yes, as a matter of fact I can. But that would make him skip important evolutionary steps, and you'd be sorry later."

Sometimes I find myself in a pit of loneliness or anti-creativity, feeling trapped in some bleak life situation, or feeling that I have taken on some piece of work so large and many-faceted that if I lived ten lifetimes I could not complete it. Part of me knows that a surprise, a breakthrough, a new element can come in at any moment and change the equation of my life. But all too often I identify myself as a part (an ego, a solidified self) that sees only what is apparent and feels trapped in it. The demands of daily life and my own expectations seem to allow me no time and no room to maneuver. I am tempted to grasp for an easy outcome, a magic potion, a distraction, or else a way to drop the whole thing.

At such times we can create tremendous doubt about the value of our life and art. Such unbelief, and the hypnotic power of self-doubt, has a real effect. We must do some mental housecleaning, collect every negative statement that we have ever made to ourselves and thoroughly burn them up, and then allow a generous interval of time for the ashes

147

to settle. Out of the ashes of doubt and the alchemy of surrender, we begin again to awaken to a faithful attitude.

A faithful attitude is a workmanlike attitude, which becomes possible when we drop into a state of *samadhi.* Otherwise our consciousness of time, whether it be tomorrow's deadline or the limits of our life span, can cheapen or vulgarize our effort. The workmanlike attitude is inherently nondualistic—we are one with our work. If I act out of a separation of subject and object—*I,* the subject, working on *it,* the object—then my work is something other than myself; I will want to finish it quickly and get on with my life. Built right into this interpretation of reality are the creative blocks and the obstacles our life interposes between subject and object; automatically they are experienced as frustrations rather than challenges. But if art and life are one, we feel free to work through each sentence, each note, each color, as though we had infinite amounts of time and energy.

Having this lavish, abundant disposition toward our time and our identity, we can persevere with a steady and cheerful confidence, and thus accomplish infinitely more and better. This is why some people are able to be more productive under pressure; the pressure itself paradoxically plunges them into a state of heightened concentration in which ordinary clock time disappears. Other people may work best in an almost monastic setting, where they can suspend their normal lives for a lengthy season and go to a quiet place in the country to do their work. These people may attain the state of steady, patient, and faithful concentration only when they are so generous with their time that mere weeks or months vanish in the steady growth of the work and the learning. Faith, then, is the inner dimension of patience.

The necessary equation of patience with faith arises because we cannot drop out of the world to undergo the growth and do the work needed—whether for hours or for years—unless we trust that "Spirit stands still long enough."

In our rapidly changing world there is no objective basis for this trust, other than the knowledge that other people have done it and come through. We simply have to have it, crazy as it may seem at times: faith in the rightness of our aim, in the ultimate fittingness of the obstacles, tests, and lessons that present themselves along the way, in the integrity and mystery of our own evolution.

We have been saying all along that improvisation in life and art means moment-to-moment nonstop flow, experiencing and creating each moment as it comes; but the opposite is also true. It is equally important to step back from time and have a look at our life and art from the long view, from perspectives that telescope large amounts of space and time.

Once in Granada, the ancient capital of Moorish Spain, I walked with a friend through an out-of-the-way quarter of the old city. We stumbled into a towering old church that was being restored. The place, once majestic, was a dusty, debris-strewn construction site. We climbed over sawhorses and began talking with the lone workman, a short, sturdy fellow named Paco. He was stringing the church with electricity. He said that they had burned oil lamps in the church for centuries; the smoke had blackened the walls (we could vaguely discern the outlines of frescoes all over the walls and alcoves underneath the soot and grime). He then said that after he fixed the lighting he was going to repair all the stonework; then all the woodwork; then he was going to repaint all the frescoes. It became clear that this fellow in blue overalls was no ordinary workman. I said to him, "That should take you quite a long time, yes?" He answered that he could work at it every day until he was ninety, and if he didn't finish it, someone else would.

Often we are struck by the difference between the solid, substantial buildings of the past and the hideous, ticky-tack structures of the present. In the field of fine arts, we still make beautiful things; but most everyday objects around us—

roads, bridges, buildings, furniture, utensils that used to also involve art and craftsmanship—seem to be built in the easiest and cheapest way. I am convinced that this difference is related to our much speedier and more trivial view of time, and our equation of time with money. If we operate with a belief in long sweeps of time, we build cathedrals; if we operate from fiscal quarter to fiscal quarter, we build ugly shopping malls. The ugliness of many modern artifacts is not due to plastics and electronics being inherently uglier than stone or wood, and it is not because people are stupider than they used to be. It's due to the detached nonrelation between the people and the things. The artificial separation of work from play also cleaves our time and the quality of our attention. The attitude of faith says that I and my work are one, and we are organically immanent in one bigger reality. This is not possible when we live according to one reality from nine to five and another after dark. When work and play are not one, when work and worker are not one, when self and environment are not one, then quality becomes an irrelevancy, a frill; and presto—we fill the world with ugly places and things.

Some artists will rework a piece for half a lifetime before they know it is finished. An improviser may have to practice for years before being able to play a totally spontaneous minute of music in which every detail is right for its own fleeting moment. The great scientists and scholars are not those who publish or perish at any cost, but rather those who are willing to wait until the pieces of the puzzle come together in nature's own design. The fruits of improvising, composing, writing, inventing, and discovering may flower spontaneously, but they arise from soil that we have prepared, fertilized, and tended in the faith that they will ripen in nature's own time.

Ripening

After periods during which one has actively tried to solve a problem, but has not succeeded, the sudden right orientation of the situation, and with it the solution, tend to occur at moments of extreme mental passivity. . . . A well-known physicist in Scotland once told me that this kind of thing is generally recognized by physicists in Britain. "We often talk about the Three B's," he said, "the Bus, the Bath, and the Bed. That's where the great discoveries are made in our science."

WOLFGANG KÖHLER

When the flute master comes to town at the beginning of our story, he plays a small, simple piece on his instrument. Everyone's mouth hangs open in wonder, and the oldest man present says that this musician plays like a god. Then the student goes off to study with him. He does everything perfectly, but he's not playing like a god, he's playing like a competent professional musician. He dutifully pursues his training until he reaches the dead end of his competence and brilliance. When pushed beyond his limits he encounters frustration, suffering, and disappointment. He hits a kind of nadir, impoverished and drunk, and then lives through a long fallow period. Then, after all his calamities, he plays the same old piece he had played a thousand times before, but somehow the way he plays it is different—now he's got soul.

Something gave up in him that was standing between him and his soul. He's got soul now, but the story is not about acquiring soul, because we come equipped with soul from the start. The inevitable price exacted by experience is that all kinds of obscuration, noise, fear, and forgetting get interposed between us and our true self, and we can't see it any more. Almost by surprise, after he has given up hope, he can play with soul, he can play *as* soul. The story, then, is about the ripening of soul.

The annals of art and science are full of stories of men and women who, desperately stuck on an enigma, have worked until they reached their wit's end, and then suddenly made their longed-for creative leap or synthesis while doing errands or dreaming. The ripening takes place when their attention is directed elsewhere.

Insights and breakthroughs often come during periods of pause or refreshment after great labors. There is a preparatory period of accumulating data, followed by some essential but unforeseeable transformation. William James remarked in the same vein that we learn to swim in winter and skate in summer. We learn that which we do not concentrate on, the part that has been exercised and trained in the past but that is now lying fallow. Not doing can sometimes be more productive than doing.

Sooner or later we are guaranteed to come to a crisis or impasse. We suffer through a period of intense buildup of pressure, during which we may come to feel that we are at the end of our rope, that there is simply no way to solve the problem. We have to become hopelessly stuck. Likewise, the alcoholic, the addict, the procrastinator usually has to "hit bottom" before he or she can have the insights that will lead to recovery.

Sometimes I feel that I have wasted a whole day trying one tactic after another to make my tools work, to make a single paragraph come out, to play a single authentic-sounding musical stroke. At a later time, the problem solves itself easily. Feeling like a fool, feeling obsessed with something that can't turn out, is simply a stage in solving the problem. Creative despair feels rotten when it overtakes us, but it is necessary—it is a symptom that we are throwing our whole being into the problem.

In science, we sit face to face with the perpetual gap between nature's mysterious data and our capacity to know them and frame them. In art we face the same gap, between our half-intuited feelings and imaginings and our capacity to know them and frame them—T. S. Eliot's "undisciplined squads of emotion." The creative moment arrives when we jump that gap, revive the dead zone.

The creative surprise often takes place when the pressures come off in an episode of relaxation or surrender. Walt Whitman spoke in this light of the value of loafing. But relaxation here does not mean indolence or lethargy; it means an alert, poised equilibrium, attentive, ready to shift in any direction with the movement of the moment. We feel with some excitement and trepidation that we are onto something, though we don't yet know what it is. Often the spiritual and aesthetic epiphanies come just when we are seemingly unemployed. Discussing the power of mistakes, we saw that in life, as in a koan, we get to the point where interruptions are the answer. Attending to the interruption frees us to see our original situation freshly and find the alchemical gold in it. This ingredient of the creative process includes not only incubation and ripening but the hypnotic technique of *redirection of attention* ("Look *there!*"), and while you are looking, you have transformed what is *here*.

When you have lived with a creative problem for a while, you begin to see it and label it as a problem. It is no longer fresh. Then you're stuck with it; the problem ties you up in knots. It becomes a vicious circle. Any attempt to force the situation causes it to rigidify further. But if you put the whole project aside and try something new, you don't know

of any problem. You can do the new project without thinking of your problem. Mysteriously, you find that there are
ways of working out even the most heartbreakingly knotty
enigmas when you are not constantly on top of them. *La
siesta,* mindfully employed and gainfully enjoyed, can be a
powerful instrument of spiritual awakening.

Perhaps the most radical sociopolitical invention of the
past four thousand years was the sabbath. The practice of the
sabbath (if we ignore the incrustation of rules and regula-
tions imposed by organized religions) recognizes that we
need space and time reserved from the rushing and pressures
of everyday life, reserved for going inside ourselves, for rest,
review, and revelation.

Trusting yourself releases conscious defenses to allow
the unconscious integrations to become manifest. This is also
the process of therapy, allowing people to relax their defenses so they can respond from a deeper source in themselves. The systole-diastole of effort and relaxation sets the
stage for the luck of the well prepared.

Recalling the example of the Weber-Fechner law, the
mind that is tied up in investment and attachment is a mind
that has fifty candles burning and will not notice the fifty-first
when it is lit. When we surrender, we can relax into a more
subtle, sensitive mind that has few candles burning, or even
none. Then when the creative surprise flares up, it can be
seen clearly and distinctly, and, most important, it can be
acted upon.

The hundredth and final koan from *The Blue Cliff Record*
asks, "What is the blown-hair sword?"—meaning, what is
the sword (the mind-sword, the heart-sword) so sharp that if
you merely blow a hair against the blade it will be cut in two?
What is the cutting edge of the present moment?

Pa Ling's answer: "Each branch of coral supports the
moon."

Imagine yourself standing by the seashore in moonlight, looking down at the wet coral glistening. The moonlight reflects from the coral to your eyes at the speed of light, which on the human scale means instantaneously. There is direct transmission with no impediment, and the whole moon is available from every part of the coral, like a hologram. Every one of those thousands of sparkles is a complete image of the whole. The way to have and to be a sharp, powerful instrument is to be minutely sensitive, and use that sensitivity to see the epiphanies that have been sitting around you all along. "Not I," says D. H. Lawrence,

> not I, but the wind that blows through me!
> A fine wind is blowing the new direction of Time.
> If only I let it bear me, carry me, if only it carry me!
> If only I am sensitive, subtle, oh, delicate, a winged gift!
> If only, most lovely of all, I yield myself and am borrowed
> By the fine, fine wind that takes its course through the
>   chaos of the world
> Like a fine, an exquisite chisel, a wedge-blade inserted;
> If only I am keen and hard like the sheer tip of a wedge
> Driven by invisible blows,
> The rock will split, we shall come at the wonder, we
>   shall find the Hesperides.
>
> Oh, for the wonder that bubbles into my soul,
> I would be a good fountain, a good well-head,
> Would blur no whisper, spoil no expression.
>
> What is the knocking?
> What is the knocking at the door in the night?
> It is somebody wants to do us harm.
>
> No, no, it is the three strange angels.
> Admit them, admit them. [44]

If we look again (after many knocks at the door), we see our experience of blockage, and the breakthroughs that may follow, as something else entirely, part of a natural ripening process. These openings are not simply a matter of rest and re-vision, but of gestation. In one phase of the process we exercise technique and try things out step by step. In another phase the conscious working of ideas sinks down and assimilates with the unconscious. Then there is the seemingly magical part of the process in which the material resurfaces, enriched and ripened by its unconscious sojourn. It is not, of course, the material that resurfaces; it is we who resurface, more ripe and ready to *bear* the material.

At the actual moment when free play breaks through, we no longer know or care about any of these phases; the playing plays itself.

In the art of teaching, we recognize that ideas and insights need to cook over a period of time. Sometimes the student who is least articulate about expressing the ideas is in fact the one who is absorbing and processing them most deeply. This applies as well to our own private learning of our art form; the areas in which we feel most stuck and most incompetent may be our richest gold mine of developing material. The use of silence in teaching then becomes very powerful.

Dreams, when we pay attention to them, appear as another source of deep information. Creative people, even when sleeping, are working and playing on their questions. Life is full of surprises when we're asleep. There is something in us constantly wanting to come out, and it seems to emerge more easily when we let go of the strictures (hope and fear) of consciousness. We discover that an inexplicable subterranean growth has occurred within us.

Like a birth, creative expression bursts out, of its own accord, when you and it are ripe:

My belly is as wine which hath no vent;
it is ready to burst like new bottles.
I will speak, that I may be refreshed;
I will open my lips and answer.[45]

"Spirit always stands still long enough," Minor White told us earlier, but it may not always seem so to the artist "It has chosen." Our flute player applies himself with patience and perseverance, but eventually gives up. Unbeknownst to him, the momentum of all his practice carries through, unconsciously, during the dark night of the soul.

In dealing with unconscious mind, we're dealing with an ocean full of rich, invisible life forms swimming underneath the surface. In creative work we're trying to catch one of these fish; but we can't kill the fish, we have to catch it in a way that brings it to life. In a sense we bring it amphibiously to the surface so it can walk around visibly; and people will recognize something familiar because they've got their own fish, who are cousins to your fish. Those fish, the unconscious thoughts, are not passively floating "down there"; they are moving, growing, and changing on their own, and our conscious mind is but an observer or interloper. That is why Jung called the depths of the unconscious the "objective psyche."

In *The Secret of the Golden Flower,* Jung writes of the Taoist masters:

What then did these people do in order to achieve the progress that freed them? As far as I could see they did nothing (*wu wei,* inaction), but let things happen, for as Master Lu Tzu teaches in our text, the Light circulates according to its own law, if one does not give up one's accustomed calling. The art of letting things happen, action in non-action, letting go of oneself, as taught by Meister Eckhart, became a key to me with which I was able to open the door to the "Way." The key is this: we must be able to let things happen in the psyche.

For us, this becomes a real art of which few people know
anything. Consciousness is forever interfering, helping, correcting, and negating, and never leaving the simple growth
of the psychic processes in peace. It would be a simple
enough thing to do, if only simplicity were not the most
difficult of all things.[46]

Does the poem exist before it is written? Does the idea
exist before it is known? Definitely! Where do we go to listen
to the music that has not yet been heard? There is a place in
our body to which we can turn and listen. If we go in there
and become quiet, we can start to bring the music up. Re-
membering Socrates and the slave: Socrates' questions develop or ripen the slave's latent knowledge.

Said Chuang-Tzu, "To a mind that is still, the whole
universe surrenders."[47] The essential feature of this state is
that we reach a point of having nothing to gain and nothing
to lose. It is like the meditation of the ex-prince Gautama
Shakyamuni, who wandered and struggled for years, passion-
ately, to attain insight and transcend birth-and-death, who
studied desperately and fruitlessly with all sorts of spiritual
teachers, who practiced self-denial and asceticism oblivious
to every discomfort—all to no avail—and who finally, during
one such bout of practice, stood up and shook the whole

thing off and had a good meal. Then he sat down again in meditation and vowed never to get up until the great change came up within him. This total surrender, letting go of needs and time, letting go as well of pretensions to holiness, abstinence, artful mind, or ideas of enlightenment, freed him to "just sit,"[48] forever if need be—just sit, still and empty, and when the morning star showed forth, he suddenly had his moment, he experienced the absolute surprise of liberation and became the Buddha, the One-who-woke-up.

The two activities we observed at the beginning of this chapter—first the stuffing of consciousness with knowledge and then ripening it in the unconscious—can occur as one, just as in improvisation judgment and free play occur as one. We are still under the thumb of the rational ego when we say that to be creative you first have to stuff consciousness with data and problems, then let them cook in the unconscious. That says that creativity (making unconscious wisdom available to consciousness) is a special or paranormal phenomenon. But what if we just drop the rational filter entirely and turn our problems over to the unconscious at once? That, after all, is what the pelicans were doing in their graceful flight over the shore just now. They do this naturally, because the life of animals is pre-conscious, pre-personal; they live in what Rilke called "the undeciphered world."[49] The accomplishment of the Buddha was to achieve this same grace, as a conscious person. Such transconscious awareness, awakening to and flowing with life in real time, can ripen in any one of us.

The
Fruits

Eros and Creation

Music, the word we use in our everyday language,
is nothing less than the picture of our Beloved. It is
because music is the picture of our Beloved that we
love music.

HAZRAT INAYAT KHAN

The beloved is already in our being, as thirst and
"otherness." Being is eroticism. Inspiration is that
strange voice that takes man out of himself to be
everything that he is, everything that he desires:
another body, another being. Beyond, outside of me,
in the green and gold thicket, among the tremulous
branches, sings the unknown. It calls to me.

OCTAVIO PAZ

Integral to the creative process is the ecstatic feeling that Walt Whitman celebrates when he says, "I sing the
body electric."[50] When play is free and skill is ripe, we are
making love making music making love making music.

Music (and I mean here the music of music, the music
of poetry, the music of creative living) plays in the mind in
a place where sexuality and sensuality play. Eros—the divine
principle of desire and love—surges from our deepest evolutionary roots: the urge to create, to generate new life, to
regenerate the species. It is the creative energy immanent in
us as living beings. "Energy is the only life, and is from the
Body; and Reason is the outward bound or circumference of
Energy. Energy is Eternal Delight."[51] This delight is the
fountain of strength and generativity released when we free

163

ourselves from the judging spectre and expand that outward circumference.

This power is symbolized in such figures as the Greek Pan and the Hindu Krishna—both of them flute-playing gods, trickster gods, lover gods, whom the ancients worshipped as symbols of cosmic vitality and free play. They represent the power of *lîla* to harness the elemental energies: the pagan, the wild, the chthonic. Their role in the inner life of the artist is to activate us in creating work that is both uninhibited and skilled, that uses the devices of culture and training and refinement to plunge us into an awareness of the source of our own being. This *lîla* is the instrumentality for hypnotically drawing people into deeper and more sacred areas of the psyche. We feel this quality of entrainment when we are carried away, or rather carried inward, by the rhythmic, mantic qualities of music, poetry, theater, and ritual.

Writing, playing, composing, painting; reading, listening, looking—all require that we submit to being swept away by Eros, to a transformation of self of the kind that happens when we fall in love.

Krishna's musical *lîla* is a sound that is irresistibly charming. He arouses and fascinates everyone around, yet he represents the strongest moral force in the world.[52] In the myths he is depicted as the seducer of the village cowgirls of Vrindavana. He simply plays his flute and they come running. According to one tale he made love to 16,000 of them in a night—godlike powers of love and generativity without doubt! In this mythic world there is no dualism between body and spirit; the visceral and spiritual passion of the god's seduction goes far beyond our ordinary, limited view of sexual passion. This seduction is what is experienced by some people, for example, who give up their professions and their security to go into the theater, because their love is the theater. This seduction is a call, a sense of vocation, art for love's sake. When we encounter the spiritual passion of Desire with a big D we are corralling all of our resources—intellectual, emotional, physical, imaginative, the animal and the angelic—and pouring them into our work.

The word *desire* comes from *de-sidere,* "away from your star." It means elongation from the source, and the concomitant, powerful magnetic pull to get back to the source. In the Sufi view, the beloved is the friend we love, while the Beloved is the Friend, God; and they are one. Love is a state of resonance between absence from and nearness to the beloved, a vibratory, harmonized resonance between being two and being one. In the art of archery the desire of the arrow and the target to be together is such that they are, in the mind of the master archer, already one.[53] In the same way, a fine baseball outfielder is already one with the ball long before he catches it. The archer is practicing a kind of *intelleto* every time he draws the bow, feeling the interpenetration of self and object, self and tool; *seeing* the identity of the moment of longing, the moment of preparation, and the moment of fulfillment.

A moment comes when we realize that we have fallen in love with our instrument, our sculptor's tools, our dance floor, our computer. We are in love with music, art, literature, cooking, physics. We feel love of beauty, love of the craft well done, love of the material, of the instruments. We feel the sensuality of playing, and of listening, reading, seeing, learning. The desire to learn and to play, if we have it at all, the motive power of creation, is part of our innate makeup, that craving to reach beyond ourselves.

Why do we do art? There may be multiple and serious motivations, such as opening people's eyes to injustice or saving the world; but if the activity to save the world doesn't give us joy, what's the point of having a world, and how will we have the wholeness and energy to carry on? This whole adventure of creativity is about joy and love. We live for the pure joy of being, and out of that joy unfold the ten thousand

art forms and all the branches of learning and compassionate
activity.

The child's instinctual desires to do, to be the cause, to
explore, to arrange things, evolve into deeper passions later
in life. Such are the ripened passions of someone who has
already experienced some suffering, fought through some of
the obscurations and disappointments, and come back to the
art form, to a renewal of creativity. Then the drive to create
is not just the entrancing magic of the child's fascination;
there is the erotic fascination, involving both love and tension, the complex dance of push and pull. It is like the complex dance of coming back to an old love.

Eros invariably embodies not only closeness but tension.
In an erotic relationship there is intimate contact and intimate risk. Falling in love with beauty or with someone else's
artwork that touches us is easy. We can experience the rapture of it and go home. But falling in love with our instrument or with our work is much more like falling in love with
a person, in that we experience the rapture and delight of the
discovery, but then we are saddled with the effort of fulfillment, with love's labors and the hard lessons in which illusions are stripped away, in which we confront difficult pieces
of self-knowledge, in which we have to stretch our physical,
emotional, intellectual stamina to the limits, in which our
patience and our ability to persevere and transcend ourselves
are tested.

A momentous and mysterious factor that keeps us going
through every obstacle is the love of our unfinished work.
"The whole difference between construction and creation,"
wrote G. K. Chesterton, "is this: that a thing constructed can
only be loved after it is constructed; but a thing created is
loved before it exists."[54] A thing constructed is a product of
mere consciousness; we see all of it. But in creation we are
pulling and being pulled in an erotic union with powerful,

deeper patterns still emerging from unconsciousness. We cannot see our unborn creation, we cannot know it, but we know it is there and we love it; and that love drives us to realize it.

The work in progress can be experienced much as another person with whom we interact, whom we get to know. We begin to have conversations with our unborn creation. We can ask it questions, and it will give us intelligible answers. Like loving someone, commitment to the creative act is commitment to the unknown—not only the unknown but the unknowable.

This Desire is more than pleasure or joy; it is a reach for the unknown. Desire grows artwork out of us in order to see itself. We are reaching out beyond the known edges of our self to incorporate Other, to touch, to sense, to reshape, to rejuvenate, to make new life. Perhaps the most ambitious piece of performance art yet undertaken was the series of Apollo missions to the Moon, which produced those extraordinary photographs of the whole Earth. We as humanity were reaching out to be able to see the symbol of our own yearning to reach out. The mind of the maker in us seeks out symbols that more and more completely express our own wholeness.

Twirl the radio dial. Most of what you hear is song after syrupy song about romantic love. This seems to be something that people never tire of hearing about. It seems to be vitally important to us.

Why? The experience of love is as close as most of us get, after childhood's end, to feeling that we are not bound by our skin, that the circumference of self can be moved or penetrated or dissolved in union with another. The ego is the outward bound or circumference of the person; it is the skin the psyche presents to the world. Our surrender to love is a touching of skin to cancel out that boundary. It is a taste of

that delightful, mystical transcendence of selfhood. In our compartmentalized, alienated society there is such tremendous hunger for union, for grounding, for surrender. We turn our intimate side toward that loved person and open a free back-and-forth exchange. In love, we disappear. We stop the world, we stop being two selves, and become an activity, an open field of sensitivity.

Love (of the beloved and the Beloved—and the pain of elongation from either) teaches us that we are part of something bigger than ourselves, part of a big System or Being. Love is where we learn the really big lessons of attachment and loss.

When Eros leads us to expansion of the self, it merges

into the other aspect of love, compassion. Compassion is the ability to relate to and identify with what we see, hear, and touch: seeing what we see not as an *it* but as part of ourselves.

Though love is a material act (whether sexual love, friendship, parenting, or any other kind of devotion, love is always an act), it lifts us out of the ordinary world into a kind of mystic participation with one another. We tune, more and more finely, our capacity to sense the other person's subtleties. We are willing to be infinitely patient and persevering. In a sense, genius equals compassion, because both involve the infinite capacity for taking pains. The great lovers, the great world reformers and peacemakers, are those who have passed beyond their individual ego demands and are able to hear the cries of the world. The motive is not self-gratification, but gratification of a bigger being of which we are part. Genius and compassion signify a transcendent, painstaking thoroughness and attention to detail—taking the trouble to take care of our own body and mind and everyone else's body and mind.

This is exactly what we do when we set out on the adventure of loving another human being. We learn, the easy way or the hard, to cultivate receptivity and mutual, expressive emancipation.

Can we transfer this receptivity, compassion, and free flow of mind to everyone and everything we touch?

Quality

It don't mean a thing
if it ain't got that swing.
DUKE ELLINGTON
IRVING MILLS

While driving to dinner with a friend, I described some of my hopes for this book: that it would help people ignite their own creativity, that it would affirm their inalienable right to express their deepest imaginings in whatever media seemed best. When we arrived at the restaurant, my friend waggled his finger sternly at me and said that he hoped my attempts to facilitate creative expression would not end up filling the world with mediocre poetry readings, boring concerts, trashy films, and putrid paintings.

I found myself plunged into considering a whole set of questions that I think we must ask but cannot answer: What is quality? What is good? The engima of quality in art brings up another word, which is to some extent out of date and therefore a bit quaint-sounding, namely, *beauty.* Our Pandora's box pours out yet more enigmas: grace, integrity, truth. What does "creative" mean? Do we use the same word to describe a dedicated Sunday painter as we use to describe a Leonardo da Vinci? When we are creating in a hitherto unknown form—and even more so when improvising—how do we recognize when it is the real McCoy? How do we know whether or when we are fooling ourselves? What is it that calls forth the aesthetic response, and how do we test it? How do we point our gyroscope?

What I have to say about quality may seem very unsatisfactory, because I will not and cannot define it; yet I insist that there is such a thing and that it is of vital importance.

Free play must be tempered with judgment, and judgment tempered with freedom to play. We perform innumerable balancing acts, dances between opposite poles, each of which is necessary for life and art to exist. We have to live right on the balance point of an equi-*valence* between free flow of impulse and constant testing and questing for quality. With too little judgment, we get trash. With too much judgment, we get blockage. In order to play freely, we must disappear. In order to play freely, we must have a command of technique. Back and forth flows the dialogue of imagination and discipline, passion and precision. We harmonize groundedness in daily practice with spiritedness in daily stepping out into the unknown.

This is another of life's rhythms of systole-diastole, like the alternating contraction and relaxation of muscles, which must be neither rigid nor flabby but in a state of *tonus.* In the instinctive life of the body, these balancing acts are performed automatically. If you're standing on one leg, the brain will decide if you're falling to the right or the left. You don't have to decide or intellectualize it; the counterbalance is set up automatically, in real time. If I am in tune and in tonus, I can step through the creative act with the assurance and spontaneity of the child, knowing that my self-balancing sense of quality will keep me on course.

Needless to say, there are multiple views of reality, innumerable definitions of what is good or valuable or beautiful, differing from person to person and moment to moment for each person. An artwork may contain material that is ugly or harsh, yet profoundly move us. An artwork may be exquisitely made, carry sensual loveliness, and express truth, yet it may be insipid.

There are infinitely many ways to structure art and as many ways to construe it once it exists. One mark of a great

poem, novel, symphony, or painting is that innumerable in-
terpretations are generated—different people see it differently, and the same person sees it differently from one time
to another. The hundredth time I taste an artwork I love, I
still find something new in it, because I am different, and
because there is some largeness or manyness in the art that
can resonate with the changing versions of myself.

Rather than beauty or quality, it is perhaps better to
speak of the beauties, the qualities. There are formal beauties, emotional beauties, essential beauties. Formal beauty
has to do with symmetry, proportion, harmony of the parts—
though *what* symmetry, *what* proportion depend on the style
and desire of the artist. In a beautifully constructed concerto
or a beautifully flowing improvisation, every note has its own
place. Every tone in a piece of music, every word in a piece
of literature interrelates with the others, the complete con-
sort dancing together. Qualities of improvisation are penetration, absorption, resonance, flow. Qualities of composition are symmetry, branching, segmentation, wholeness,
tension of opposites.

When do sounds equal music? What distinguishes a
Bach canon, or Messiaen's *Oiseaux,* or real birdsong, from
sounds we might call less musical? When each sound answers
a question posed by some other sound in the total group,
when each larger grouping of sounds answers the other
groupings, when the field of sounds both questions and answers the field of thought and emotion in us (both listeners
and players), then we have music. That is, the multilayered
aggregate possesses wholeness and integrity. Music is a conscious act that resembles the patterning of a living thing
which, not limited by consciousness, evolved over long ages.
We can see in the music, as in the organism, segmentation,
branching, symmetry, spiraling, unity amid intricate diversity. We can see the compactness, economy, completeness,
consistency, and open-endedness in its organization. These

are structural, formal qualities, but they are not abstract. Because we ourselves are living organisms, we feel them with our whole body.

Formal beauty is also the beauty of skill. The mathematician's ideal of elegance, the quality of nothing wasted, nothing needed, is what we recognize in the flight of hawks and pelicans, in the movements of athletes and dancers, as grace. Note—and this is one of the essential tensions—that elegance (economy of expression) is the opposite of galumphing (the profligacy of nature and imagination). Both tendencies contribute to the artfulness of our work.

Having whatever qualities "quality" might possess, an act might be skilled, entertaining, and impressive yet still not be art. For art there needs to be a linkage of material that is partly conscious and partly unconscious, a linkage to the emotional reality that is the shared experience of both artist and audience.

Again we reiterate that beauty need not be beautiful or pretty. One can think of many films, theater pieces, and paintings that unreservedly depict horror or ugliness, political repression, or torture—such as Picasso's *Guernica* or Pontecorvo's *Battle of Algiers*—yet they are beautiful.

There are the beauties that portray and ignite emotions. There are the beauties that portray and ignite ideas. But deeper than these (here we think perhaps of Bach) are the beauties that evoke the ground of being, against which emotions and ideas play as ephemera. By some alchemy we drop into direct mystic participation in aliveness or being itself, which is beyond emotion, skill, thought, or imagination. This is the view of mystics who see beauty as the One shining through the ten thousand things that are before our eyes. This direct expression of life itself cannot be analyzed or defined, but when we experience it, it is beyond any doubt. A person can be intellectually or emotionally involved in what he is doing, imaginatively involved, physically involved, but the real authenticity we recognize is when the person is totally involved. It is this that the old man recognizes when he whispers, "Like a god!"

Quality, beauty, play, love, numinosity cannot be defined, but they can be recognized. They are recognized when our being resonates with the object. We are beings with a little consciousness and a lot of unconsciousness, including the personal unconscious, the collective unconscious, the billion-year history encoded in and as our bodies. Artworks, dreams, events that touch us deeply play across the liminal interface between conscious and unconscious reality. They are about the exchange or, perhaps, are themselves the medium of exchange between the little that we know and the much that we are. We cannot define what is good or beautiful because definition belongs to the relative and tiny realm of rational consciousness. But when we set up our total selves as antennae or resonators, we can detect it. We are back to the enigma of play. No one can define play, but everyone, at the zoo, can tell you when a monkey or an otter is playing.

We cannot define quality, but just thinking about it raises the ante in the exploration we are undertaking here, as it did for our flute player. We assume that he was a brilliant young musician, he was technically perfect, had practiced and mastered the craft of music, had a rich inner life and powerful motivation. But there was "something lacking," and that indefinable something was quality. The master would not say what was lacking because he *could* not say. Quality is undefinable to the master as well. The student had to find out for himself, from his own being. Any knowledge he gets from someone else is not his own. The knowledge, the art, has to ripen of its own accord, from his own heart.

We find ourselves weeping at certain moments in movies or plays, even in so-called artless ones, when something in them has "struck a chord." This metaphor is exact, because

it refers to the phenomenon of resonance or sympathetic vibration. If you stroke a violin string, and there is another violin in the room, the second will resonate, will sing out on the same tone as the first. When we feel resonance it is the sure symptom of identity with the thing that sings. Quality is recognition of what Gregory Bateson called "the pattern which connects."[55]

There is something biological about art and the recognition of beauty or quality, and I don't mean by this that beauty is natural as opposed to artificial. Highly technological, abstract, or computerized art forms may carry just as much of the mysterious quality of aliveness as a landscape or a haiku. By "biological" I mean that since we are beings with all the interconnected loops and complexities and dynamics and self-reproducing flow and unconscious grace entailed by life, we are rich enough and old enough to resonate or sympathetically vibrate in the presence of something else, which is in *its* own way alive. When art is alive it sympathetically resonates with the heart. When knowledge is alive it sympathetically resonates with the deep structure of the world.

There is a Jewish tale about a famous rabbi who prayed beautifully. His words reflected a lifetime of learning and a fervent heart; they were musical, and they held deep understanding, passion, and compassion. These were quality prayers. One high holy day in his temple, his prayers reached a real epiphany of depth and intensity. At that minute, an angel landed, and said, "By the way, you pray pretty well, but over in Such-and-such village there's a fellow named So-and-so who prays better than you do." The rabbi was somewhat flustered, but he was determined to meet and if possible learn from this So-and-so. At the first opportunity, he made the journey to Such-and-such village and asked for his man. He was directed to a house, and there he met an illiterate tradesman. The rabbi asked if there was another man named So-and-so in this village. The fellow, nervous and obsequious, said no. The rabbi turned to leave, thinking he had been misled, but at the door he turned and asked the man how he had prayed at the last holy day. The man said, "I was surrounded by the prayers of the learned, the skilled, the artful, and felt so stupid, so incapable; I can't even read. All I know are the first ten letters of the alphabet. So I said to God, 'All I have are these ten letters; take them and combine them however you want so that they smell good to you.'"

This man, having only his ten letters, surrenders them and opens himself up as a resonator to the beauty and truth that lie beyond him. All knowledge, all art, is at best a partial glance from one angle or another. Passing beyond knowledge and artfulness, he resonates with a living whole and becomes himself whole.

This whole enterprise of improvisation in life and art, of recovering free play and awakening creativity, is about allowing ourselves to be true to ourselves and our visions, and true to the undiscovered wholeness that lies beyond the self and the vision we have today. That is what quality is all about: truth. Now we can see the meaning of Keats' famous line "Beauty is truth and truth beauty—that is all ye know on earth and all ye need to know."[56]

If the art is created with the whole person, then the work will come out whole. Education must teach, reach, and vibrate the whole person rather than merely transfer knowledge. Again, the flute student had to find out for himself, from his whole being. There is inevitably something lacking in books and other methods of teaching that stress procedures and information, even though they may contain tricks and steps that are valuable. The steps, the how-to's (remember here that consciously reviewing the steps of bicycle riding can make us fall off) may teach some of the classical or formal aspects of quality and beauty, which reside in the parts and their harmonies. But the romantic or mystic view that sees quality as a symptom of the One shining through is inherently not breakable into steps or qualities; it arises instead from a whole-body and whole-soul resonance with the art we are seeing or making. In improvisation in life and art, we hold these two ways of doing, seeing, and being in our two hands; we *make* and *sense* with both of them.

Quality can be compromised when the gyroscope of our inner knowing, integrating so many dynamic balancing acts, is pulled off center. We can be pulled away from ourselves, from our own resonator in the belly, toward a limited idea of what others want or toward a limited idea of what we want. The first results in attempts to be accessible, the second in attempts to be original.

One of the most insidious kinds of pressure to which an artist can succumb is the pressure to be accessible. Well-meaning advisors may tell you that x is accessible, marketable, popular, and so on, and there may indeed be artists who naturally do x out of their own being and become popular and wealthy. But if you alter your work to be more x-ish, people will spot it as inauthentic; it will not be heartfelt x because it does not originate in your own being. By all means develop and revise your work to communicate more and more clearly; but if you alter one word in order to please some imagined market "out there," the integrity and originality of everything you do is at risk. You get off the sure base of what you really know and are. Whereas if you create your own material in your own way, developing artwork that is more and more authentically yours, people will spot it as genuine. In resisting the temptation to accessibility, you are not excluding the public; on the contrary, you are creating a genuine space and inviting people in.

Ideally, artist and audience are close, interresponsive, accessible to each other's minds and hearts. But in a world of mass economics and mass communication, producers and middlemen of all kinds insist that our work conform to a lowest common denominator. Natural communication between artist and audience is simulated by the banalities of market research and advertising. This is a particularly insidious process because it arises not from anyone's bad intentions but from the fundamental nature of large systems and institutions. The danger to the artist is that under pressure of these institutions he might internalize those demands and replace his immaculate, natural voice with an artificially synthesized one.

On the other hand, if we self-consciously try to be original, we can wander in the opposite direction, going for a distinctive voice or look that sets us apart from everybody else. Young artists easily fall into the trap of confusing originality with newness. Originality does not mean being unlike the past or unlike the present; it means being the origin, acting out of your own center. Out of your spontaneous heart you may do something reminiscent of the very old, and it will be original because it will be yours. Under the spell of wanting to appear original, you may end up rejecting your first thoughts and dredging up something far out—not yourself. (If we try for the Tao, the koan goes, we move away from it.) Yet the first thoughts are the ones that, by definition, are the inspired ones. Just stay with the obvious and humdrum. Because you are the unique product of evolution, culture, environment, fate, and your own quirky history, what is obvious and humdrum to you is guaranteed to be thoroughly original. The great scientific, artistic, and spiritual discoveries generally involved some breathtaking piece of obviousness that everyone else had heretofore been too scared or too hidebound by conventional wisdom to see or imagine. Some unwieldy, overcomplicated thought structure, like the epicycles of mediaeval astronomy, comes crashing down to reveal a synthesis so simple "a child could have thought of it."

Paradoxically, the more you are yourself, the more universal your message. As you develop and individuate more deeply, you break through into deeper layers of the collective consciousness and the collective unconsciousness. There is no need to alter your voice in order to please others, and no need to alter it in order to differentiate yourself from others. Quality arises from, and is recognized by, resonance with inner truth. Hence the famous prayer of Socrates: "Beloved Pan and all ye other gods who haunt this place, give me beauty in the inward soul; and may the outward and inward man be one."[57]

Art for Life's Sake

*It is difficult
to get the news from poems;
yet men die miserably every day
for lack
of what is found there.*
WILLIAM CARLOS WILLIAMS

Artists used to be able to talk convincingly about creating something for posterity, about making things that would live on and even grow for hundreds of years past the death of their makers. Duration has traditionally been one of the great measures of quality.

But right now the world's future seems a bit doubtful. With vast amounts of weaponry all around us; with air, water, soil, and cities becoming more toxic every year; with the whole of Earth's life-support systems at risk, we don't have a clear guarantee that there *will* be much posterity. For years many of us have wondered and talked about what we can do to see that a world and a civilization still exist, to see that there's someone to make art for and with; and we have participated, each in our own way, in innumerable projects aimed at helping to heal the situation as each of us saw it.

Often we find that our attempts to fix things only end up by making them worse. Part of the impasse is that in dealing with an intricately interconnected network of patterns on the scale of the global ecology, neither our reasoning faculties nor our feeling faculties are equal to the job. The only capacity our species has that is powerful enough to pull us out of this predicament is our self-realizing imagi-

nation. The only antidote to destruction is creation. The
game we are now playing is for keeps; this is an age that
may see us either go down the drain or create a whole new
civilization. Precisely because the standing of posterity is so
tenuous, art is now more relevant than it has ever been.
And again, I mean not just art but artfulness: playfulness,
seriousness, connectedness, structure, wholeness. And
heart.

So the issues raised in this book also point toward some
activity beyond individual creativity, beyond art. Let us call
it the Imaginary Liberation Front. Not art for art's sake, but
art for life's sake.

This means an explosion of creativity into areas of life
where it has been largely excluded. Looking at international
politics, looming multiple ecological and economic catastro-
phes, resurgences of fundamentalist fanaticisms and racisms,
it is fair to say that conventional logic and conventional ideas
have brought us to an impasse. What can pull us out is the
fresh perception fostered by a creative attitude, as well as
openness to the free play of possibilities. In politics more
than in any other sphere of life, what most clogs creativity is
fear. What we see behind the seeming impossibility of humans to make peace among ourselves or with the planet that
nurtures us is a kind of rigidity, freezing us into outmoded
categories and frames of reference. This is why totalitarian
states and fundamentalist religions make it their first order of
business to restrict free speech, art, film, and other avenues
of expression and communication. Humor in particular is
anathema in such settings.

Looking at the state of the planet, we can easily see that
only major breakthroughs will pull us through. Miracles.
What is needed in the coming generation is a whole series
of adaptive, creative, evolutionary jumps. Everything we
know about individual art making indicates that creative

breakthroughs are possible, not as extraordinary messianic events but as a matter of course. When we relax the five fears and replace compulsion with practice, stretching the moment of inspiration, then creative breakthroughs can become reliable everyday facts of life.

There is a saying, "We have met the enemy, and they is us." Indeed we must realize this in order to survive. But it is equally true, and equally necessary, to say we have met the great composers, the great creators—and they is us too.

Creative inspiration is not the property only of certain special people like professional artists. To give away our creative ability to professional artists is like giving away our healing ability to doctors. The professionals are vitally necessary, as repositories of knowledge, tradition, resources, and most of all as catalysts to the healing power that is within us. But the real healing, the real creativity, is done by us, and we abrogate that power at our own peril. Sir Herbert Read writes, "The aesthetic view of life is not confined to those who can create or appreciate works of art. It exists wherever natural senses play freely on the manifold phenomena of our world, and when life as a consequence is found to be full of felicity."[58]

There are two notions linked here: creativity extended into more moments of time; creativity extended into the lives of more people. Neither spectators nor victims, we can be directly involved in the making of ourselves and our world. There are no prescriptive solutions, no grand designs for grand problems. Life's solutions lie in the minute particulars, involving more and more individual people daring to create their own life and art, daring to listen to the voice within their deepest, original nature, and deeper still, the voice within the Earth.

Creativity arises from play, but play is not necessarily linked to values. Commitment and love are. There is not *a* creative process. There are many creative processes, with many layers, many levels of involvement and intent. Contemplative mystics work on the self only. Artists wrapped up in the art world work on material only. In either case, there is a separation of values and the sacred from life. But in the Imaginary Liberation Front, artists work on the self and material together, in an alchemy of sympathetic resonance.

What we usually call creativity involves such factors as intelligence, ability to see the connections between formerly separated facts, ability to break out of outmoded mindsets, fearlessness, stamina, playfulness, and even outrageousness. Very creative people can use these capacities in highly conventional fields. They can be used for good or evil. Creativity can be manifested in medicine, in propaganda, in teaching poetry, in designing a house or an atom bomb. Unfortunately, the same capacity for play and experiment that gives rise to our finest achievements has also resulted in the invention of ever more refined methods of mass destruction that may negate millions of years of evolutionary achievements.

The drive to create is yet another factor, different from creativity. It characterizes someone who is driven to do something from the depths, something that he or she feels must be done regardless of whether it's popular or well rewarded by society. This inner compulsion to realize a vision depends on creativity for its fulfillment, but it is not the same as creativity. The inspired poet or musician may in fact be less creative, less clever, adept, or original than the designer of an advertising campaign, but he is motivated by a life-or-death need to bring the vision into being. Even this passionate need to create, however, is not necessarily linked with values. Perfectionists are not necessarily compassionate or beyond ego. A physicist may be just as obsessed with solving a problem as a composer, yet either one's work may

result in a bomb. And there have been genius writers, like
Rimbaud, who toss off masterpieces and then give up art
because it bores them.

Beyond the drive to create is yet a deeper level of commitment, a state of union with a whole that is beyond us.
When this element of union is injected into our play-forms,
we get something beyond mere creativity, beyond mere purpose or dedication; we get a state of acting from love. Love
has to do with the perpetuation of life, and is therefore
irrevocably linked to deeply held values.

I have never ceased to be astounded at the power of
writing, music making, drawing, or dance to pull me out of
sadness, disappointment, depression, bafflement. I am not
talking about entertainment or distraction, but of playing,
dancing, drawing, writing my way through and out. This
process resembles the best in psychotherapy. We don't go
away and avoid the troubling thing, but rather confront it in
a new framework. The capacity to personify, mythologize,
imagine, harmonize is one of the great mercies granted in
human life. We are thus able to conceptualize the unknowns
of the psyche, to work with forces in us which, if left unconscious, would overwhelm us. That is the magic of poetry. It
uses words to communicate that which words cannot communicate. When you run into problems in our artwork, you may
think you are working out the creative problem; but in-
directly you are working out other life problems as well. This
healing power works in the other direction too. If, like
Picasso, you occupy yourself with working out the problem
of how to express a world of feeling in blue paint, you are
also working out something else. What is that something
else?

We cannot define it or understand it, but we can do it.
Zen master Dogen, in the thirteenth century, said, "To study
the Buddha Way is to study the self. To study the self is to

forget the self. To forget the self is to perceive oneself as all things. To realize this is to cast off the body and mind of self and others. When you have reached this stage you will be detached even from enlightenment, but will practice it continually without thinking about it."[59]

Living myths continually surface. In 1988, three whales were trapped under the Alaska ice, and for two weeks the world's attention was focused on those whales and the efforts of men and ships to cut a path of holes in the ice pack and enable the whales to escape to open sea. Finally, two of the whales made it. The intense concentration of cameras and reporters during that time transformed the event into a kind of global window on the improvisational theater of everyday life. The situation was dramatic, unpredicted, and unscripted, with known limits but an unknown course and unknown outcome, played out in real time, contained in a defined space or *temenos,* connected with powerful symbols.

Improvisational theater does not necessarily take place in a theater and does not necessarily involve people who call themselves actors or artists. The materials of improvisational theater, art, music, dance are all around us all the time. But when, as in the case of the whales, our attention goes fully into and with the event, with a sense of empathy and spiritual involvement, the difference between art and life is bridged.

Creativity, like life, is a recursive process, involving interactive, interlooping circuits of control and nourishment between organism and environment. If the organism is, like us, conscious, it may feel that it is the tool (or even the victim) of some big mysterious force. But there is no *force*— there is the interconnectedness of the big system, Gaia. Biologists, historians, and other scholars are developing an increasingly substantial foundation for the Gaia hypothesis,[60] which recognizes that the Earth is in fact a single living organism.

Since rational, materialistic epistemology came to define the direction of Western culture in post-Renaissance times (with roots going far back into antiquity), we have progressively denied the reality of those processes that relate *(re-ligio)* us to context and environment—namely, art, dreams, religion, and other roads to the unconscious. Gregory Bateson has shown how art, religion, and dreaming are necessary remedies for correcting the inherent narrowness of conscious purpose.[61] That healing element (in whatever field our creative act takes shape) is to learn to address the world in a way that comprehends the unconscious totality, the inherent paradoxes: "not just pretty poetry, but the glue, the *logic* upon which living things are built."[62] Art, music, poetry, paradox, sacrament, theater are the very medicines we need, yet they are the very things our modern minds drop by the wayside. Plato, in the *Timeas,* speaks of the arts of theater and ritual as our essential ally in the recovery of our lost wholeness:

> The motions akin to the divine part of us are the thoughts and revolutions of the universe. These every man should follow, correcting those circuits in the head that were deranged at birth, by learning to know the harmonies and revolutions of the world; he should assimilate the thinking being to the thought, renewing his original nature.[63]

The ultimate source and destination of creative work lies, then, in the wholeness of the psyche, which is the wholeness of the world. Hence, the healing properties of art. Integration with the natural order, or big Self, is to rediscover, reveal oneself in context, in nature, in balance, to liberate the creative voice. This essence is with us all the time, but since

it's usually covered up we're usually sick. When we uncover our essence, we're also recovering from the sickness of the spirit.

I said at the beginning of this book that we have an inalienable right to create, and that, if anything, would be the credo of the Imaginary Liberation Front. I would like to say too that we have a right to a beautiful and healthy world. But this is not so; art and a beautiful world are made by hard work and free play. They are not rights but privileges. We have the right to work, to earn it. Our work links art and survival, art and healing, art and social change. There is a linkage between the urge toward beauty, the urge toward health, the urge toward political freedom.

The obstacles to human freedom, community, and creativity are to be absorbed and transcended in the full humanization of the person. Culture and the arts are a vital resource for survival. Creation, in the arts, science, technology, and daily life, is a primary source of human realization. Creativity can replace conformity as the primary mode of social being.

The free play of creativity is not the ability to arbitrarily manipulate life. It is the ability to experience life as it is. The experience of existence is a reflection of Being, which is beauty and consciousness. Free play is that which makes this experience accessible to the individual. The goal of freedom is human creativity, the enhancement and elaboration of life. Creativity always involves a certain amount of discipline, self-restraint, and self-sacrifice. Planning and spontaneity become one. Reason and intuition become two faces of truth.

We now find ourselves, as individuals, as nation-states, and as a species, involved in a period of intense and often bewildering transformation. The systems of government, production, culture, thought, and perception to which we have become accustomed and that have functioned for so long are not working. This presents us with a challenge. We can cling to that which is passing, or has already passed, or we can remain accessible to—even surrender to—the creative process, without insisting that we know in advance the ultimate outcome for us, our institutions, or our planet. To accept this challenge is to cherish freedom, to embrace life, and to find meaning.

Heartbreakthrough

The artist's life cannot be otherwise than full of conflicts, for two forces are at war within him—on the one hand the common human longing for happiness, satisfaction and security in life, and on the other a ruthless passion for creation which may go so far as to override every personal desire. . . . There are hardly any exceptions to the rule that a person must pay dearly for the divine gift of creative fire.
CARL JUNG

The freedom to create is a fruit of personal growth and evolution. In the creative life cycle we pass through at least three stages: innocence (or discovery), experience (or the fall), and integration (or rejuvenation or mastery). Birth, blockage, and breakthrough. This passage is not, of course, a single and straight line; developmental phases are complexly shifting and interlooping throughout our lives.

In our original state of innocence, creativity evolved out of the child's primary creative experience of *disappearing*—pure absorption in free play. But eventually we experience life's battles, the long list of evils that seem to come intrinsically woven into our existence on earth, as well as the internal impedimenta of fear and judgment. Sometimes before we can reach a breakthrough to clarity we live through a dark night of the soul, as did our flute player. Sometimes we are able to transcend innocence-and-experience and achieve a renewed innocence. The mature artist comes back around, spiral fashion, to a state that resembles child's play, but which has been seasoned by the terrors and trials it took to get there. At the end of the journey "costing not less than every-thing," writes T. S. Eliot,

> *We shall not cease from exploration,*
> *And the end of all our exploring*
> *Will be to arrive where we started*
> *And know the place for the first time.* [64]

The breakthrough, the moment of return, is the *samadhi* of reorganized innocence. With his very life at stake every time he picks up his tools, the artist can do his real work only by recovering his original mind-of-play, which has nothing to gain and nothing to lose.

There is a unique moment, which we may or may not reach, when we take back all the introjects and spectres, take responsibility for our acts, and cut the Gordian knot. Then the difficulties and barriers drop away and we have a clear, unobstructed transmission. This transmission is, in the full sense, a mystery, in that while it is lucidly obvious when it happens to us, it must be experienced to be believed. The effect is metabolic rather than conceptual. A kind of *fanà* has taken place; we disappear and become a carrier wave, a vehicle for the music that plays us. The power of creative spontaneity develops into an explosion that liberates us from outmoded frames of reference and from memory that is clogged with old facts and old feelings. Addiction, procrastination, and fear are blown away by this carrier wave, and our music becomes a message about big Self.

This is when we are able, finally, to disappear. Virginia Woolf, in this connection, weaves an interesting parable around our ignorance of Shakespeare's life (his known biography would fill not more than three pages).

For though we say that we know nothing about Shakespeare's state of mind; even as we say that, we are saying something about Shakespeare's state of mind. The reason perhaps why we know so little of Shakespeare—compared with Donne or Ben Jonson or Milton—is that his grudges and spites and antipathies are hidden from us. We are not held up by some "revelation" which reminds us of the writer. All desire to protest, to preach, to proclaim an injury, to pay off a score, was fired out of him and consumed. Therefore his poetry flows from him free and unimpeded. If ever a human being got his work expressed completely, it was Shakespeare. If ever a mind was incandescent, unimpeded, I thought, turning again to the bookcase, it was Shakespeare's mind.[65]

The vicious circles, the judging spectres, society's defenses against creativity, the inherent frustrations and disappointments of life, none of these obstacles can be controlled or conquered, because, as we have seen, the very idea of control or conquest is a dualistic, us-and-them attitude that invites the obstacles back in another form. But they can be absorbed and harmonized when we put ourselves in relation to a higher, deeper power. The liberation, the awakening to creativity, comes when we can finally see ourselves as neither placating nor resisting the universe, but seeing our true relation to it, as part to whole.

Frank Herbert has a character in *Dune* say, "Once a man has become one thing he will die rather than change into its opposite."[66] But this is not necessarily true. It is possible to make the big jump, to die to the self-clinging ego, and still remain alive and healthy on this earth. The old myths of Creation refer not to some fictitious event in 4004 B.C. but to something that we can do right here in this body. The imagination is our true self, and is in fact the living, creating god within us. The myths of resurrection refer not to the undoing of physical death but to a transformation we can effect right now, a rebirth into Self. Henry Miller writes of this turning point:

My life itself became a work of art. I had found a voice, I was whole again. The experience was much like what we read of in connection with the lives of Zen initiates. My huge failures were like a recapitulation of the experience of the race: I had to grow foul with knowledge, realize the futility of everything, smash everything, grow desperate, then humble, then sponge myself off the slate, as it were, in order to recover my authenticity. I had to arrive at the brink and then take a leap in the dark.[67]

The formula for creation is simple. Just identify our impedimenta, and set them down, like setting down an overburdened suitcase that we have been carrying for far too long. If we are free and unperturbable, like the clouds, then whatever creation is in us will flow out, naturally and simply. It's as easy as saying, "Let there be light." But the easiest thing to say can be the hardest to practice. We desperately cling to *it,* whatever *it* may be for us, cling to our thought of gaining it, avoiding it, or keeping it once we have it. There is no refuge, salvation, or vacation from it, for the simple reason that we carry it with us wherever we go. We have our hands full with our own limited and limiting conception of selfhood.

The secret is to *drop it*—whatever *it* may be. This is not deprivation but enrichment. It is dropping off hope and fear and letting our much vaster, simpler, true self show through, letting ourselves be ambushed by the great Tao that moves forever through this world.

The ultimate issue for the creative artist is how this turning point, this moment of transformation through surrender, is reached, and how it works to potentiate and instill life into one's creative voice.

> Chao-Chou once asked Nan-Chuan, "What is the Tao?"
> Nan-Chuan answered, "Your ordinary mind is the Tao."

"Should we try for it or not?" asked Chao-Chou.

"If you try to direct yourself toward it, you go away from it," answered Nan-Chuan.

Chao-Chou continued, "If we do not try, how can we know that it is the Tao?"

Nan-Chuan answered, "Tao does not belong to knowing or to not-knowing. Knowing is illusion; not-knowing is stupor. If you really attain the Tao of no-doubt, it is like the great sky, so vast and boundless. How, then, can there be right and wrong in the Tao?" At these words, Chao-Chou was suddenly enlightened.[68]

A later master, Mumon, explained this famous incident in these words:

Hundreds of flowers in spring, the moon in autumn,
A cool breeze in summer, and snow in winter;
If useless things do not hang in your mind,
Every season is a good season for you.[69]

The violin bow moves across thirteen inches of string, the paintbrush moves across the blank confines of the canvas: infinite play in a limited space. It moves until the meaning is manifest in both the fine detail and the total gestalt. That movement and meaning must be new and fresh, must reaffirm the eternal verities, must entertain and delight, must be completely self-contained yet open-ended. But we can play on for a thousand years and never totally fulfill these demands. Anyone who wants to express meaning in symbols and words, in music, in paint, has got to have a taste for impossible tasks, a willingness to tolerate great frustration, a touch of Quixote. This may involve a passionate and sometimes terrifying commitment to see our play-forms through to their conclusion in spite of all obstacles.

Beethoven at the age of thirty-two realized that he

would never recover his hearing, and even worse, foresaw the loneliness and emotional isolation that was in store for him. He wrote his despairing, premature will, the Heiligenstadt Testament, in those same summer weeks as he wrote the *Second Symphony,* that incomparable study of light, air, and happiness. He was later to write of this time: "If I had not read somewhere that a man may not voluntarily part with his life so long as a good deed remains for him to perform, I should long ago have been no more."[70] The *Eroica Symphony,* one of the revolutionary conceptual and emotional leaps in the history of art, arose from Beethoven's synthesis of the vastly conflicting states of mind that were forced upon him at this time. Beethoven is so often described by his contemporaries as dreadfully unfortunate, misanthropic, alternately resigned to and defiant of fate. Yet it is precisely because he chose the path of surrender, of despair transcended, that Beethoven, this wild man, this deaf man, lives on among the greatest poets of joy the world has ever known.

There is nothing that can stop the Creative. If life is full of joy, joy feeds the creative process. If life is full of grief, grief feeds the creative process. Examples of jail art abound, the most famous of which is *Don Quixote.* e. e. cummings wrote *the enormous room* while incarcerated in a dirty, crowded French jail during World War I. Olivier Messiaen composed *Quartet for the End of Time,* one of the greatest accomplishments of twentieth-century music, while in a Nazi concentration camp. Messiaen sat in Stalag VII in Silesia in the bitter winter of 1941 and created eight movements of, in his words at the time, "unfailing light, of unalterable peace." We have seen again and again how immense can be the power of limits, the power of circumstance, the power of life's pull in generating original breakthroughs of mind and heart, spirit and matter. It's wonderful to retire to a mountaintop and paint pretty pictures. But more wonderful and more challenging still is for the artist to sit right in the midst of the karmic struggle, all the sufferers of all times and places hanging on his brush—and then with full awareness to pick up that brush and, like Hakuin, draw "nothing but" a circle. Such a circle will be treasured for centuries as a door of perception, a door to liberation. The least mark on the paper becomes an act of supreme courage in which the suffering of the artist and his world are alchemized into something quite different, a thing of beauty and wonder.

When this alchemy fully ripens within us, our acts of improvisation in life and art take on all the manifold dimensions of *lîla;* innocence and experience fuse, and we are free to play like a god.

Notes

Publication data for note entries are in the Bibliography.

Attributions for chapter opening quotations

page   1   Ranier Maria Rilke, sonnet number 3 in *The Sonnets of Orpheus,* 1922.

page   4   From Whitney Balliet: "Profiles: Stéphane Grappelli." *The New Yorker,* 19 January 1976.

page 17   William Blake, in "The Pickering Manuscript," [1803] 1989.

page 25   Martha Graham, in Agnes de Mille, *Dance to the Piper,* 1951.

page 31   W. B. Yeats, *Last Poems and Plays,* 1940.

page 36   Frances Wickes, *The Inner World of the Child,* 1928.

page 42   Carl Jung, *Psychological Types,* 1923.

page 51   Aaron Copland, *Music and Imagination,* 1952.

page 59   Vincent van Gogh, *Further Letters to His Brother,* 1888.

page 66   Igor Stravinsky, *The Poetics of Music,* 1942; *The Blue Cliff Record,* number 80, [1128] 1977.

page 78   Jallaludin Rumi, *The Mathnavi,* [1260] 1981.

page 88   Miles Davis, no source; M. C. Richards, *Centering,* 1962.

page 94   Gregory Bateson. From a conversation with the author.

page 102   Lu Chi, *Wen Fu: The Art of Writing,* 261 A.D.

page 115   Rollo May, *The Courage to Create,* 1975.

page 126   Gustave Flaubert. From a letter to Louise Colet.

page 133   William Blake, *Jerusalem,* 1806.

page 140   Edgar Dégas, "Notebooks 1856," in *Artists on Art,* 1945.

page 147   Minor White, *Rites & Passages,* 1978.

page 152   Wolfgang Köhler, *The Task of Gestalt Psychology,* 1969.

page 163   Hazrat Inayat Khan, *Music*, [1921] 1960; Octavio Paz, *The Bow and the Lyre*, 1973.
page 170   Duke Ellington and Irving Mills, no source.
page 181   William Carlos Williams, "Asphodel, That Greeny Flower," in *Journey to Love*, 1955.
page 191   Carl Jung, *Modern Man in Search of a Soul*, 1933.

Text Notes

1. This story was discovered by Trevor Leggett, in *Zen and the Ways*, 1978.
2. William Blake, *The Marriage of Heaven and Hell*, 1793.
3. Arnold Schoenberg, "Brahms the Progressive," 1933, in *Style and Idea*, 1950.
4. Emmanuel Winternitz, *Leonardo da Vinci as a Musician*, 1985.
5. Karl Czerny, [1800], in O. G. Sonneck, ed., *Beethoven: Impressions By His Contemporaries*, 1926.
6. Baron de Trémont, [1809], in ibid.
7. William Blake, *The Marriage of Heaven and Hell*, 1793.
8. e. e. cummings, *1 x 1 [One Times One]*, 1944.
9. Hakuin, "Orategama," [1748], in *Zen Master Hakuin*, 1971.
10. Chang Chung-yuan, *Creativity and Taoism*, 1970.
11. Blaise Pascal, *Pensées*, 1670.
12. Johan Huizinga, *Homo Ludens: A Study of the Play Element in Culture*, 1938.
13. Stephen Miller, "Ends, Means, and Galumphing," in *American Anthropologist*, 1973. "Galumphing" after Lewis Carroll, *Through the Looking Glass*, 1896.
14. W. Ross Ashby, *Introduction to Cybernetics*, 1956.
15. Gospel According to Matthew 4:4.
16. Alexander Pope, *Essays on Criticism, Part III*, 1711.
17. Paul Radin, *The Trickster*, 1956.
18. Gospel According to Mark 10:15 (King James Version).
19. Ernst Kris, *Psychoanalytic Explorations in Art*, 1952.
20. *The Blue Cliff Record*, number 80, [1128] 1977.
21. D. W. Winnicott, *Playing and Reality*, 1971.
22. Jallaludin Rumi, *The Mathnavi*, [1260] 1981.
23. Blake, *Milton*, 1804.
24. T. S. Eliot, "Little Gidding," in *Four Quartets*, [1941] 1952.

25. Rico Lebrun, *Drawings*, 1961.
26. This view of assimilation and accommodation is due to Jean Piaget. See especially his *Play, Dreams, and Imitation in Childhood.*
27. T. S. Eliot, "Burnt Norton," in *Four Quartets*, [1941] 1952.
28. Igor Stravinsky, *The Poetics of Music*, 1942.
29. Wendell Berry, "Poetry and Marriage," in *Standing by Words*, 1983.
30. Psalms 118:22.
31. Emmanuel Winternitz, *Leonardo da Vinci as a Musician*, 1985.
32. Peter Schickele, *P. D. Q. Bach on the Air*, 1967.
33. Igor Stravinsky, *The Poetics of Music*, 1942.
34. Bob Dylan, "Absolutely Sweet Marie," in *Blonde on Blonde*, 1966.
35. For a powerful exploration of these matters, see Alice Miller, *The Drama of the Gifted Child*, 1981.
36. e. e. cummings, *1 x 1 [One Times One]*, 1944.
37. K. Seelig, *Albert Einstein*, 1954.
38. Virginia Woolf, *A Room of One's Own*, 1929.
39. Aaron Copland, *Music and Imagination*, 1952.
40. William Blake, "Auguries of Innocence," in "The Pickering Manuscript," [1803] 1989.
41. Seng-Tsan, *Hsin Hsin Meng*, [eighth century] 1951.
42. Jallaludin Rumi, *The Mathnavi*, [1260] 1981.
43. *The Blue Cliff Record*, [1128] 1977.
44. D. H. Lawrence, "Song of a Man Who Has Come Through," in *Complete Poems*, 1930.
45. Job 32:19.
46. Richard Wilhelm, trans., *The Secret of the Golden Flower*, with commentary by Carl Jung, 1931.
47. Chuang-Tzu, *The Way of Chuang-Tzu*, [fourth century B.C.], trans. Thomas Merton, 1965.
48. Kigen Dogen, "Shikantaza," in *Shobogenzo*, [1250] 1975.
49. Ranier Maria Rilke, *Duino Elegies*, [1922] 1961.
50. Walt Whitman, *Leaves of Grass*, 1855.
51. William Blake, *The Marriage of Heaven and Hell*, 1793.
52. David Kinsley, *The Sword and the Flute*, 1975.
53. Eugen Herrigel, *Zen in the Art of Archery*, 1953.
54. G. K. Chesterton, Preface to Dickens' *Pickwick Papers.*
55. Gregory Bateson, *Mind and Nature*, 1979.
56. John Keats, "Ode on a Grecian Urn," in *Annals of Fine Art*, 1819.
57. Plato, *Phaedrus*, trans. Thomas Taylor, 1792.
58. Herbert Read, *Annals of Innocence and Experience*, [1940] 1974.

59. Kigen Dogen, "Genjokoan," in *Shobogenzo*, [1250] 1975.

60. James Lovelock, *Gaia: A New Look at Life on Earth*, 1979, and *Ages of Gaia*, 1988.

61. Gregory Bateson, "Style, Grace, and Information in Primitive Art," in *Steps to an Ecology of Mind*, 1972.

62. Gregory Bateson, *Mind and Nature*, 1979.

63. Plato, *Timeas*, trans. Thomas Taylor, 1792.

64. T. S. Eliot, "Little Gidding," in *Four Quartets*, [1941] 1952.

65. Virginia Woolf, *A Room of One's Own*, 1929.

66. Frank Herbert, *Dune Messiah*, 1967.

67. Henry Miller, "Reflections on Writing," in *Wisdom of the Heart*, 1941.

68. Mumon Ekai, koan 19, in *Mumonkan (The Gateless Gate)*, [1228] 1967.

69. Ibid.

70. Ludwig van Beethoven, *Letters*, ed. Emily Anderson, 1961.

Bibliography

Ashby, W. Ross. *Introduction to Cybernetics.* New York and London: John Wiley and Sons, 1956.

Balliet, Whitney. "Profiles: You Must Start Well and End Well—An Interview With Stéphane Grappelli." *The New Yorker,* 19 January 1976.

Bateson, Gregory. *Steps to an Ecology of Mind.* New York: Ballantine, 1972.

———. *Mind and Nature.* New York: E. P. Dutton, 1979.

Beethoven, Ludwig van. *Letters.* Edited by Emily Anderson. London, 1961.

Bernstein, Leonard. *The Unanswered Question.* Cambridge: Harvard University Press, 1961.

Berry, Wendell. *Standing by Words.* San Francisco: North Point Press, 1983.

Blake, William. *The Marriage of Heaven and Hell.* London, 1793.

———. *Milton.* London, 1804.

———. *Jerusalem.* London, 1820.

———. "Several Questions Answered" and "The Pickering Manuscript" in *Blake, Complete Writings.* Edited by Geoffrey Keynes. Oxford: Oxford University Press, 1989.

The Blue Cliff Record. [1128]. Translated by Thomas and J. C. Cleary. Boulder and London: Shambhala, 1977.

Carroll, Lewis. *Through the Looking Glass and What Alice Found There.* London, 1896.

Chang Chung-yuan. *Creativity and Taoism.* New York: Julian Press, 1970.

Chuang-Tzu. *The Way of Chuang-Tzu,* [fourth century B.C.]. Translated by Thomas Merton. London: Unwin Books, 1965.

Copland, Aaron. *Music and Imagination.* Cambridge: Harvard University Press, 1952.

cummings, e. e. *the enormous room.* New York: Liveright, 1923.

cummings, e. e. *1 x 1 [One Times One]*. New York: Liveright, 1944.

de Mille, Agnes. *Dance to the Piper.* Boston: Little, Brown, 1951.

Dégas, Edgar. "Notebooks, 1856." In *Artists on Art,* edited by Robert Goldwater and Marco Treves. New York: Pantheon, 1945.

The Diamond Sutra. [second century]. Translated by A. F. Price. Boulder and London: Shambhala, 1969.

Dogen, Kigen. *Shobogenzo (The Eye and Treasury of the True Law).* [1250]. Translated by Kosen Nishiyama and John Stevens. 4 vols. Tokyo: Niakyamo Shobo, 1975.

Eliot, T. S. *Four Quartets.* In *The Complete Poems and Plays, 1909–1950.* New York: Harcourt, Brace & World, 1952.

Flaubert, Gustave. *The Letters of Gustave Flaubert, 1830–1880.* Edited by Francis Steegmuller. Cambridge: Harvard University Press, 1982.

Grudin, Robert. *Time and the Art of Living.* New York: Ticknor & Fields, 1982.

Hakuin. "Orategama." [1748]. In *Zen Master Hakuin: Selected Writings.* Translated by Philip Yampolsky. New York: Columbia University Press, 1971.

Herbert, Frank. *Dune Messiah.* New York: Berkley Books, 1967.

Herrigel, Eugen. *Zen in the Art of Archery.* New York: Pantheon, 1953.

Hughes, Richard. *A High Wind in Jamaica.* New York: Harper and Row, 1929.

Huizinga, Johan. *Homo Ludens: A Study of the Play Element in Culture.* [1938]. Boston: Beacon Press, 1955.

Joyce, James. *Finnegans Wake.* London: Faber and Faber, 1939.

Jung, Carl. *Psychological Types.* London: Kegan Paul, 1923.

———. *Modern Man in Search of a Soul.* Translated by Cary Baynes. London: Routledge & Kegan Paul, 1933.

Keats, John. "Ode on a Grecian Urn." In *Annals of Fine Arts.* London, 1819.

Khan, Hazrat Inayat. *Music.* [1921]. London: Barrie & Rockliff, 1960.

Kinsley, David. *The Sword and the Flute.* Berkeley: University of California Press, 1975.

Köhler, Wolfgang. *The Task of Gestalt Psychology.* Princeton: Princeton University Press, 1969.

Kris, Ernst. *Psychoanalytic Explorations in Art.* New York: Shocken, 1952.

Lawrence, D. H. *Complete Poems.* New York: Viking Press, 1930.

Lebrun, Rico. *Drawings.* Berkeley and Los Angeles: University of California Press, 1961.

Leggett, Trevor. *Zen and the Ways.* Boulder and London: Shambhala, 1978.

Lévi-Strauss, Claude. *The Savage Mind (La Pensée Sauvage).* Chicago: University of Chicago Press, 1966.

Lu Chi. *Wen Fu: The Art of Writing,* [261 A.D.]. Translated by Sam Hamill. Portland, Oreg.: Breitinbush Books, 1987.

May, Rollo. *The Courage to Create.* New York: W. W. Norton, 1975.

Miller, Alice. *The Drama of the Gifted Child.* Translated by Ruth Ward. New York: Basic Books, 1981.

Miller, Henry. "Reflections on Writing." In *Wisdom of the Heart.* New York: New Directions, 1941.

Miller, Stephen. "Ends, Means, and Galumphing: Some Leitmotifs of Play." *American Anthropologist 75,* no. 1 (1973).

Mumon Ekai. *Mumonkan (The Gateless Gate).* [1228]. Translated by Zenkei Shibayama. New York: Harper & Row, 1945. Or translated by Nyogen Senzaki and Paul Reps, in *Zen Flesh, Zen Bones.* Tokyo and Rutland, Vt.: Charles Tuttle, 1967.

Pascal, Blaise. *Pensées.* Paris, 1670.

Paz, Octavio. *The Bow and the Lyre.* [1973]. Austin: University of Texas Press, 1987.

Piaget, Jean. *The Construction of Reality in the Child.* Translated by Margaret Cook. New York: Basic Books, 1954.

———. *Play, Dreams, and Imitation in Childhood (La Formation du Symbole).* Translated by C. Gattegno and F. M. Hodgson. New York: W. W. Norton, 1962.

Plato. *Meno.* Translated by Thomas Taylor. London, 1792.

———. *Phaedrus.* Translated by Thomas Taylor. London, 1792.

———. *Timeas.* Translated by Thomas Taylor. London, 1792.

Pope, Alexander. *Essays on Criticism, Part III.* London, 1711.

Radin, Paul. *The Trickster.* Boston: Routledge & Kegan Paul, 1956.

Read, Herbert. *Annals of Innocence and Experience.* [1940]. Brooklyn: Haskell, 1974.

Richards, M. C. *Centering.* Middletown: Wesleyan University Press, 1962.

Rilke, Ranier Maria. *The Sonnets to Orpheus.* [1922]. Translated by A. E. MacIntyre. Berkeley: University of California Press, 1961.

———. *Duino Elegies.* [1922]. Translated by A. E. MacIntyre. Berkeley: University of California Press, 1962.

Rumi, Jallaludin. *The Mathnavi.* [1260]. Translated by R. A. Nicholson. 6 vols. Cambridge: Cambridge University Press, 1934. Fragments translated by Daniel Liebert. Santa Fe: Source Books, 1981.

Schickele, Peter. *P. D. Q. Bach on the Air.* New York: Vanguard Recordings, 1967.

Schoenberg, Arnold. *Style and Idea.* Berkeley and Los Angeles: University of California Press, 1950.

Seelig, K. *Albert Einstein.* Zurich: Europa Verlag, 1954.

Seng-Tsan. *Hsin Hsin Meng.* [eighth century]. Translated by D. T. Suzuki in *Essays in Zen Buddhism.* London: Rider, 1951.

Sonneck, O. G., ed. [1926]. *Beethoven: Impressions by His Contemporaries.* New York: Dover, 1967.

Stravinsky, Igor. *The Poetics of Music.* Cambridge: Harvard University Press, 1942.

Thayer, A. W. *Thayer's Life of Beethoven.* Edited by Eliot Forbes. Princeton: Princeton University Press, 1964.

van Gogh, Vincent. *Further Letters of Vincent van Gogh to His Brother.* London: Constable & Co., 1888.

White, Minor. *Rites & Passages: His photographs accompanied by excerpts from his diaries and letters.* New York: Aperture, 1978.

Whitman, Walt. *Leaves of Grass.* Brooklyn, 1855.

Wickes, Frances. *The Inner World of Childhood.* [1928]. New York: Appleton-Century, 1966.

Wilhelm, Richard, trans. *The Secret of the Golden Flower.* [eighth century]. With commentary by C. G. Jung. New York: Harcourt, Brace, & World, 1931.

Williams, William Carlos. "Asphodel, That Greeny Flower." In *Journey to Love.* New York: New Directions, 1955.

Winnicott, D. W. *Playing and Reality.* London: Tavistock, 1971.

Winternitz, Emmanuel. *Leonardo da Vinci as a Musician.* New Haven: Yale University Press, 1985.

Wolfe, Thomas. *The Story of a Novel.* New York: Charles Scribner's Sons, 1936.

Woolf, Virginia. *A Room of One's Own.* New York and London: Harcourt Brace Jovanovich, 1929.

Yeats, William Butler. *Last Poems and Plays.* London: Macmillan, 1940.

Illustrations

About the Author

Stephen Nachmanovitch is a violinist, composer, poet, teacher, and computer artist. He studied psychology and literature at Harvard and has a Ph.D. in the History of Consciousness from the University of California at Santa Cruz. As an improvisational violinist he has performed his own music internationally. In addition to live concerts and writing, he is actively involved in the field of visual music, creating videos and computer software that integrate graphics and original music. His multimedia works have involved dance, theater, poetry, photography, painting, and film. He has taught and lectured widely in the United States and in Europe, and has published in fields ranging from proto-zoology to religion. At present he is composing a large mixed-media piece called *American Zen.*